3-STEP
SLOW COOKER
COOKBOOK

3-STEP
SLOW COOKER
COOKBOOK

DELICIOUS, HASSLE-FREE HOMEMADE MEALS

DREW MARESCO

EDITOR-IN-CHIEF OF *BESTRECIPES* MAGAZINE

PAGE STREET
PUBLISHING CO.

PAGE STREET
PUBLISHING CO.

TO MY FAMILY AND FRIENDS,

THANK YOU FOR ALL OF THE ENCOURAGEMENT
AND LOVE ALONG THE WAY. YOU HELPED
MAKE THIS DREAM COME TRUE.

CONTENTS

CONTENTS (CONT.)

REAL EASY BBQ 129

VEGETARIAN DELIGHTS 143

INTRODUCTION

Since my very early years, I've had an interest in all things culinary and have loved being in the kitchen. I remember when my grandmother first sat me up on the counter, placed me right next to the mixing bowl and guided me step by step with every ingredient through my first recipe. I became Grandma's kitchen helper; we made puddings, cakes, frostings and more cookies than I can count! In the following years, I gained a greater interest in the kitchen. My love for cooking deepened and many assumed I would eventually turn it into a career.

As a young adult, I spent many weekends in the kitchen trying new recipes. Having an insatiable sweet tooth, I was making mostly desserts at that time. As I grew older and my palate gave way to more sophisticated flavors, I began to cook more savory dishes. I learned new recipes and techniques whenever and however possible, with much of my education coming from watching online videos and cooking shows on TV. Through the lives of culinary entrepreneurs like Martha Stewart and Jamie Oliver, I saw that a career in food was not only desirable, but possible. So I started a small blog, which grew into a website. Fast forward, I am now the editor-in-chief of a food magazine that I built from the ground up!

Cookbooks are written every day, and most people will make only one recipe from any given cookbook they may purchase. Why? The recipes look tantalizing and exciting but end up requiring something many don't have—time. Time is becoming more and more of a precious commodity, and most people (except for myself!) don't see cooking for hours as an enjoyable experience. The complexity and time involved made cooking a chore and not an enjoyable experience. My goal is to make creating delicious dishes simple and to bring back the joy! We all want to save time in the kitchen, but how can we do that without sacrificing quality or flavor?

The answer to this culinary question is a kitchen appliance which has all but been forgotten—the humble slow cooker. It's time to revamp our view of what this appliance can do for you. From its early days of stews and braises to modern-day meals, the slow cooker has been helping hungry cooks save time preparing their favorite dishes, but we've only begun to scratch the surface of all this appliance can do. In this cookbook, I give you a variety of recipes to make—from some of the classics to the exotic to the "I didn't know that could even be made in a slow cooker." The best part about these recipes is that each one can be made in just three simple steps or fewer. With minimal preparation, these meals are ready to eat in just a few hours—hours that you can spend outside the kitchen. What's not to love about that?

The great thing about slow cooking is that no experience is necessary! Regardless of your culinary background, you'll find that the recipes in this cookbook are approachable and enjoyable—a welcome change for anyone looking to make great-tasting meals. You're bound to find a few new favorites that you and your family will love! From my kitchen to yours, I hope you enjoy these recipes as much as I did.

Drew Maresco

NOTE: For the most part, I use a 6-quart (6-L) slow cooker. Times may vary depending on the size slow cooker you use. There are a few recipes that are not 6-quart (6-L) and cannot be changed. Each recipe specifies the exact size slow cooker needed, so read carefully for the best results!

FIX IT AND FORGET IT
COMFORT FOODS

Comfort food gives us a warm, fuzzy feeling—foods that create thoughts of family, friends, spending time in the kitchen and recipes made with love. In fact, the most comforting foods become our favorites, not so much by the ingredients or the time spent preparing, but by the memories attached to them. With such a diversity of cultural foods and cuisines from which to choose, it's easy and fun to explore different tastes and styles of comfort food that may look a bit different from the foods you ate growing up. Some of these are Southern-inspired dishes from my mom's side, while some are Depression-era foods from my dad's side. You're sure to love the recipes I've compiled here, as they are the family favorites I grew up with! You may recognize a few of your favorites as well—some with a twist and some left the good old-fashioned way!

CLASSIC PHILLY CHEESESTEAK

There's nothing quite like the classic Philly cheesesteak. This slow cooker version is spot-on and extremely easy to make.

1. Stir together the beef, onion, broth, garlic powder, salt and pepper in your 6-quart (6-L) slow cooker. Cover and cook on high for 4 hours or on low for 8 hours. For the last hour, add in the green peppers. Serve on hoagie rolls and top with sliced cheese.

1½ lbs (681 g) beef top sirloin, cut into ½-inch (1.3-cm) strips

1 white onion, sliced

1 cup (240 ml) beef broth

1 tsp garlic powder

½ tsp salt

½ tsp black pepper

2 green peppers, thinly sliced

6 hoagie rolls, sliced lengthwise, toasted

12 slices provolone cheese

1 cup (240 ml) water

1 cup (240 ml) ketchup

2 cloves garlic, minced

½ cup (120 ml) white vinegar

½ cup (110 g) dark brown sugar

¼ cup (32 g) flour, mixed with ¼ cup (60 ml) water

3 lbs (1.4 kg) beef brisket, fat trimmed

Kosher salt

3 medium onions, chopped

FALL-APART BEEF BRISKET

A Passover brisket I once had inspired this dish. It was the perfect recipe for a slow cooker! This tender brisket with homemade sauce is a real standout.

1. Stir together the water, ketchup, garlic, vinegar, sugar and flour mixture in a medium bowl.

2. Generously season the brisket with the kosher salt. Add the onions and brisket to your 6-quart (6-L) slow cooker and pour in the ketchup mixture. Cover and cook on high for 4 hours or on low for 8 hours. Serve sliced with more of the sauce poured on top.

BEEF AND RICE STUFFED PEPPERS

I love stuffed peppers. They were something our family ate often when I was growing up, so I knew that if they were going to be made in a slow cooker, they had to be just as good as Mom made them! Surprisingly, these peppers turned out tasting better than I had imagined, and I loved not having to pre-cook the rice. Timeless and time-saving!

1. Prepare the peppers by cutting off the tops, slicing the flesh from the top and throwing away the remaining stem. Remove the seeds and as much of the white pith as you can.

2. Stir together the beef, peppers, rice, ¼ cup (40 g) of the onion, half of the basil, half of the garlic, salt and pepper in a large bowl. Using your hands, mix and evenly fill the peppers and place in your 6-quart (6-L) slow cooker.

3. Stir together the tomatoes, sugar, water, remaining onion, basil and garlic in a small bowl. Pour the sauce mixture over the peppers, cover and cook on high for 4 hours or on low for 8 hours. Top with the sliced cheese just before serving.

SERVES 4

4 sweet bell peppers, any color

1 lb (454 g) ground beef—ground round is perfect here

¾ cup (139 g) uncooked Basmati rice

1 small onion, finely chopped, divided

1 tbsp (2 g) dried basil, divided

2 cloves garlic, minced, divided

1 tsp salt

¼ tsp pepper

1 (10.5-oz [298-g]) can crushed tomatoes

2 tbsp (28 g) brown sugar

¾ cup (180 ml) water

4 thick slices mozzarella or pepper Jack cheese—which cheese you use is totally up to you. I think mozzarella is more kid-friendly, but pepper Jack is my personal favorite!

1 tbsp (15 ml) oil

1 large onion, thinly sliced

Salt, to taste

3 lbs (1.4 kg) chuck roast—other roast meats can work here

Pepper, to taste

4 cups (960 ml) beef broth

3 ribs celery, diced

3 carrots, diced

Mashed potatoes, for serving

CARAMELIZED-ONION POT ROAST

Sunday afternoons, Grandma's house and the smell of a pot roast cooking in the oven go hand-in-hand in my memories. In fact, pot roast is nostalgic for many people as they reminisce on the classics made by the older generations. Our grandparents had their secret recipes, but this one is sure to become a new tradition for your family!

1. Heat the oil over medium-high heat in a large skillet. Add the onion and cook for 10 minutes, stirring constantly until browned—you are looking for pretty dark here, but not burned. Reduce the heat to medium and continue cooking the onion for 10 more minutes. Season the onion with salt, and cook for 10 more minutes; reduce the heat to low if necessary, stirring occasionally.

2. Rub the meat with the salt and pepper. Add it to your 6-quart (6-L) slow cooker with the broth, celery, carrots and caramelized onion. Cover and cook on high for 4 hours or on low for 8 hours. Serve over mashed potatoes.

SIMPLY AWESOME MEATLOAF

Meatloaf is a wonderfully classic comfort food. Whether you look back with loving memory or weren't a huge fan as a kid, I promise you, your grown-up taste buds will love this one.

1 cup (240 ml) tomato sauce or ketchup

2 tbsp (30 ml) prepared yellow mustard

¼ cup (55 g) brown sugar

2 lbs (908 g) ground beef

1 egg

½ cup (68 g) breadcrumbs—panko works well here

1½ tsp (9 g) salt

Pepper, to taste

1 small onion, finely diced

1. Whisk together the tomato sauce, mustard and sugar in a small bowl.

2. Combine the beef, egg, breadcrumbs, salt, pepper, onion and half of the tomato sauce mixture in a large mixing bowl. Using your hands—and I really do recommend using your hands or you risk over-mixing and making the final dish tough—mix together until fully incorporated. Shape the mixture into a round loaf. Carefully place it into your 6-quart (6-L) slow cooker. Cover and cook on high for 3 hours or on low for 6 hours.

3. Spoon the remaining sauce over the meatloaf, and let it rest for about 10 minutes before cutting and serving.

2 ribs celery, diced

2 carrots, diced

1 medium onion, quartered

½ head cabbage, cut into 1-inch (2.5-cm) wedges

1½ lbs (681 g) small potatoes, halved

3 lbs (1.4 kg) corned beef brisket—you can trim some of the fat off, but leave some for flavor

1 packet or 1 tbsp (2 g) pickling spice

½ tsp dried thyme

Water

IRISH CORNED BEEF AND CABBAGE WITH POTATOES

A traditional St. Patrick's Day feast, corned beef is perfect for dinner, and the leftovers make delicious sandwiches. Every year, someone asks me for a recipe, so it makes sense to include it here. A delicious Irish dinner is right around the corner! Why wait until March to feast on this tasty and easy-to-make meal?

1. Add the celery, carrots, onion, cabbage and potatoes to your 6-quart (6-L) slow cooker. Lay the brisket, fat-side up, on top. Sprinkle the pickling spice and thyme over the meat and vegetables. Add water until the brisket is almost completely covered. Cover and cook on high for 4 hours or on low for 8 hours.

2. Remove the meat and vegetables from the water, slice the meat and serve.

BEEF STROGANOFF WITH EGG NOODLES

Stroganoff has become a dish I truly love. With its tender beef, robust flavor and creamy sauce, I'm not sure how anyone wouldn't love it. Serving it over egg noodles makes it one of my favorite comfort foods, and once you've tried it, I'll bet you have a new favorite, too.

1. Place the mushrooms and onion in your 6-quart (6-L) slow cooker. Sprinkle in the flour and stir. Season the short ribs with salt and pepper and place them on top of the mushrooms and onion. Gradually pour in the broth and Worcestershire sauce, cover and cook on high for 4 hours or on low for 8 hours.

2. Cook the noodles according to the package directions. Using two forks, shred the beef, removing the bones—it sounds more tedious than it is. The meat just falls off the bone. Stir in the sour cream and mustard. Serve over noodles with fresh dill.

SERVES 6

1 lb (454 g) button mushrooms, trimmed and quartered

1 medium onion, thinly sliced

⅓ cup (42 g) flour

2 lbs (908 g) short ribs—a more economical cut of beef can be used here, like stew meat

Salt and pepper, to taste

1½ cups (360 ml) beef broth

⅛ cup (30 ml) Worcestershire sauce

12 oz (340 g) egg noodles

⅓ cup (80 ml) sour cream

1½ tbsp (23 ml) Dijon mustard

½ cup (4 g) chopped fresh dill, to serve

12 cabbage leaves

1 egg, beaten

¼ cup (60 ml) ketchup

1 small onion, finely chopped

1 tsp salt

¼ tsp pepper

1 tbsp (2 g) dried basil

2 cloves garlic, minced

1 lb (454 g) ground beef—ground round is perfect here!

¾ cup (139 g) uncooked Basmati rice

1 (14.5-oz [411-g]) can tomato sauce

¼ cup (55 g) brown sugar

¼ cup (60 ml) lemon juice

4 tsp (20 ml) Worcestershire sauce

CLASSIC STUFFED CABBAGE ROLLS

Stuffed cabbage is a classic yet often intimidating comfort food that I grew up eating, but we never made them from scratch! It was a dish our local meat market made that my mom would grab when she was strapped for time. It's hard to believe they really are so simple to make. Now I make them from scratch, and so can you!

1. Bring a large pot of water to a boil. Submerge the cabbage leaves until they are limp, for about 5 minutes. Drain the leaves and set aside.

2. Using your hands, mix the egg, ketchup, onion, salt, pepper, basil, garlic, beef and rice in a medium bowl. Use a ¼-cup (60-g) measure to scoop the meat mixture into the center of each cabbage leaf. Fold in the sides, roll the ends over and place them into your 6-quart (6-L) slow cooker.

3. Combine the tomato sauce, sugar, lemon juice and Worcestershire sauce in a small bowl. Pour over the cabbage rolls, cover and cook on high for 4 hours or on low for 8 hours.

BEEF SKILLET PIE WITH CORNBREAD

A skillet pie is perhaps a cousin to something more familiar—the shepherd's pie. This version of a skillet pie is rich and tomatoey and served with cornbread on top instead of mashed potatoes. The slow cooker steams the cornbread, making it extremely tender and the perfect complement to this comforting meal.

1. Heat the oil in a large skillet over medium-high heat. Add in the ground beef, onion and mushrooms, cooking until the beef is no longer pink and the vegetables have softened, about 5 to 7 minutes. Sprinkle the flour over the mixture and stir for about 2 minutes. Season with salt and pepper. Transfer the beef mixture to your 6-quart (6-L) slow cooker, add the peppers and stir in the tomato paste and water. Cover and cook on high for 3 hours or on low for 6 hours.

2. Stir together the cornmeal, flour and baking powder in a small bowl. Pour in the melted butter, milk, sugar and egg, stirring until the batter is smooth. Using a measuring cup, scoop the cornbread batter into the bubbling beef mixture. Repeat the process, spacing the batter mounds evenly. If cooking on low, turn your slow cooker to high, cover and continue to cook for 20 to 30 more minutes or until the cornbread is cooked through.

SERVES 6

1 tbsp (15 ml) olive oil

1½ lbs (681 g) ground round beef

1 medium onion, chopped

10 oz (283 g) white mushrooms, stems removed, thinly sliced

2 tbsp (16 g) flour

Salt and pepper, to taste

2 red bell peppers, stemmed, seeded and thinly sliced

¼ cup (60 ml) tomato paste

1 cup (240 ml) water

CORNBREAD DUMPLINGS

1 cup (122 g) yellow cornmeal

1 cup (125 g) flour

2 tsp (9 g) baking powder

1 tbsp (14 g) butter, melted

¾ cup (180 ml) milk

3 tbsp (38 g) sugar

1 egg

3 lbs (1.4 kg) beef chuck roast, cut into 1-inch (2.5-cm) cubes

5 medium carrots, peeled and sliced into ½-inch (1.3-cm) diagonals

4 medium red potatoes, peeled and cut into ¾-inch (1.9-cm) cubes

16 oz (454 g) fresh mushrooms, quartered—mini bellas or button mushrooms work well here!

1 large yellow onion, chopped

3 cloves garlic, minced

4 cups (960 ml) low-sodium beef broth

3 tbsp (45 ml) tomato paste

2 tbsp (30 ml) Worcestershire sauce

¼ cup (27 g) sweet paprika—not the smoked variety or this dish won't be edible!

¼ cup (55 g) brown sugar

2 tsp (4 g) ground mustard

2 tsp (6 g) kosher salt, or to taste

½ tsp pepper

Loaf of crusty bread, sliced, for serving

HUNGARIAN GOULASH

You may look at this recipe and think, "Where are the noodles?" If so, you are thinking of American Goulash! Introducing Hungarian Goulash—a stew that uses quite a lot of paprika and looks quite different from its American counterpart. Flavor-packed and loaded with hearty vegetables, this is a real stick-to-the-ribs dish. Serving this up with some crusty bread is a must!

1. Place the beef cubes in your 6-quart (6-L) slow cooker. Add the carrots, potatoes, mushrooms, onion and garlic around the meat.

2. Whisk the broth, tomato paste, Worcestershire sauce, paprika, sugar, mustard, salt and pepper in a medium mixing bowl. Pour the mixture into your slow cooker. Cover and cook on high for 4 hours or on low for 8 hours. Serve with a warm slice of bread.

WHOLE "ROASTED" SPICED CHICKEN WITH RED POTATOES

2 tsp (12 g) salt
2 tsp (5 g) paprika
1 tsp onion powder
1 tsp thyme
1 tsp pepper
½ tsp cayenne pepper
½ tsp garlic powder
4½-lb (2-kg) whole chicken
1½ lbs (681 g) red potatoes, quartered
1 (14.5-oz [411-g]) can chicken broth

I am a sucker for a rotisserie chicken. I wanted to come up with a simple recipe that delivered that same unique flavor but without the fuss. I believe this recipe does just that. And if you have any leftovers, this makes a great chicken salad!

1. Stir together the salt, paprika, onion powder, thyme, pepper, cayenne pepper and garlic powder in a small bowl. Rub the spices over the chicken, place in a resealable bag and refrigerate for 5 hours or overnight.

2. Place the potatoes in your 6-quart (6-L) slow cooker, pour in the broth and place the chicken on top. Cook on high for 5 hours or on low for 10 hours.

3. Carefully transfer the cooked chicken to a roasting tray and broil to crisp the skin. Serve with potatoes.

4 carrots, peeled and chopped

3 ribs celery, chopped

1 medium onion, chopped

1 tsp black peppercorns

1 bay leaf

1 sprig fresh thyme

1 tbsp plus 2 tsp (14 g) kosher salt

4-lb (1.8-kg) whole chicken

8 cups (1.9 L) water

POACHED WHOLE CHICKEN

Poaching chicken is not only healthy, but keeps the meat as moist as it can be. The benefit of doing this in your slow cooker is you can place the entire chicken in the pot—no need to spend extra money on an already separated chicken, or spend time doing it yourself. And don't even think about getting rid of that cooking liquid as you now have the perfect base for a fantastic chicken noodle soup! Check out the recipe for Classic Shredded Chicken Noodle Soup (page 117) in the By the Spoonful chapter.

1. Add the carrots, celery, onion, peppercorns, bay leaf, thyme and salt to your 6-quart (6-L) slow cooker—a smaller slow cooker will be too small for this. Place the chicken on top, breast-side up, and pour in the water, adding more if the chicken isn't covered or almost fully covered. Cook on high for 3 hours or on low for 6 hours, until the chicken reaches an internal temperature of 165°F (74°C).

2. When the chicken is fully cooked, carefully lift it out of the slow cooker and let it rest for 20 minutes, then carve it into portions. Discard everything but the stock, then pour it through a fine-mesh strainer—for the clearest stock, line the fine-mesh strainer with cheesecloth before straining.

BRAISED CHICKEN THIGHS WITH RICE

Chicken and rice may not sound super exciting, but this is so flavorful and easy that you'll be making it again and again as a staple comfort food. Make sure you use the cooking liquid to make the rice so it's one less step in your already busy day and one step closer to your dinner!

1. Add the onion, carrot, celery, garlic, chicken, wine, bay leaf, rosemary, thyme, broth, salt and pepper to your 6-quart (6-L) slow cooker. Cover and cook on high for 4 hours or on low for 8 hours.

2. If cooking on low, increase the heat to high, stir in the rice and let cook for 30 more minutes. Remove the bay leaf before serving.

NOTE: *If you cannot add the rice before this dish is fully cooked, remove the chicken from the slow cooker once done, transfer the cooking liquid to a medium saucepan and bring it to a boil. Add the rice and reduce the heat to low, cooking covered for 20 minutes or until the liquid is absorbed and the rice is tender.*

SERVES 6

1 medium onion, finely diced

1 large carrot, finely diced

1 rib celery, finely diced

2 cloves garlic, minced

2 lbs (908 g) bone-in, skinless chicken thighs—can use boneless, but I find bone-in brings out the best flavor

¾ cup (180 ml) white wine or vermouth

1 bay leaf

2 tsp (2 g) dried rosemary

¼ tsp dried thyme

1½ cups (360 ml) chicken broth

Salt and pepper, to taste

1 cup (185 g) uncooked Basmati or other long-grain rice

2 (15-oz [425-g]) cans
chicken broth

2 tbsp (4 g) dried basil

Zest of 1 lemon

1 lemon, juiced

½ tsp salt

¼ tsp pepper

3 tbsp (42 g) butter

2 lbs (908 g) boneless,
skinless chicken thighs

1½ cups (252 g)
uncooked orzo

Fresh basil, for garnish,
optional

LEMON BASIL CHICKEN WITH ORZO

Deliciously fresh and slightly tart, this recipe has all the workings of a perfect weeknight meal. Cooking the orzo right in the slow cooker makes this a no-muss, no-fuss dinner.

1. Stir together the chicken broth, dried basil, lemon zest and juice, salt, pepper and butter in your 6-quart (6-L) slow cooker. Add the chicken to the broth mixture, cover and cook on high for 3 hours or on low for 6 hours.

2. Remove the chicken from your slow cooker and onto a plate using a slotted spoon. If cooking on low, turn your slow cooker to high, stir in the orzo and add the chicken back into your slow cooker, cover and cook for 20 more minutes. Garnish with fresh basil if using.

COQ AU VIN BLANC (WINE-BRAISED CHICKEN)

Even time-pressed cooks can have a couple French dishes in their repertoire! Although the title sounds fancy, this recipe is really quite simple . . . but invite your guests over and let them believe it was difficult—I won't tell, if you won't!

1. Using some cotton kitchen twine, tie the thyme, parsley and bay leaf into a bundle and add to your 6-quart (6-L) slow cooker.

2. Heat 1 tablespoon (15 ml) of the oil to medium-high in a large skillet. Season the chicken generously with salt and pepper. Working in batches to avoid crowding, cook the chicken, skin-side down, until the skin is golden brown, for about 4 minutes, and add to your slow cooker. Add the remaining 1 tablespoon (15 ml) of oil, onion, carrots and garlic to the skillet and cook for 4 minutes, until the onion softens. Stir in the tomato paste and flour, cooking for 1 more minute. Add the wine and simmer for 1 more minute and pour into your slow cooker. Cover and cook on high for 4 hours or on low for 8 hours.

3. Remove and discard the herb bundle. Cook the couscous according to package directions. Serve the chicken and sauce over couscous sprinkled with fresh parsley.

SERVES 4

3 sprigs fresh thyme

3 sprigs fresh parsley

1 bay leaf

2 tbsp (30 ml) oil, divided

4-lb (1.8-kg) whole chicken, cut into 6 to 8 pieces and patted dry

Salt and pepper, to taste

1 medium onion, halved and thinly sliced

3 medium carrots, sliced crosswise on the diagonal into ½-inch (1.3-cm) pieces

2 cloves garlic, minced

3 tbsp (45 ml) tomato paste

⅓ cup (42 g) flour

1 cup (240 ml) dry white wine

2 cups (346 g) couscous

Chopped fresh parsley, for serving

LEMON AND OLIVE CHICKEN TAGINE

Comfort foods look different around the globe, and it's fun to give other flavors and cuisines a try without spending an entire day in the kitchen. While the sound of a recipe containing raisins, olives and cinnamon may sound very strange to you, it's a common Moroccan combination! Give it a try!

1. Stir together the garlic, cumin, ginger, paprika, salt, pepper, cinnamon, turmeric, onion and oil in a large bowl. Add the chicken thighs and toss.

2. Transfer the chicken mixture to your 6-quart (6-L) slow cooker. Add the lemon, olives and raisins on top. Cover and cook on high for 3 hours or on low for 6 hours.

3. Prepare the rice according to package directions. Serve the tagine over the rice, topped with parsley and cilantro.

SERVES 6

4 cloves garlic, minced

1 tsp ground cumin

1 tsp ground ginger

1 tsp sweet paprika

1 tsp salt

½ tsp pepper

½ tsp ground cinnamon

¼ tsp powdered turmeric

1 large onion, grated

2 tbsp (30 ml) oil

2 lbs (908 g) boneless, skinless chicken thighs

½ fresh lemon, thinly sliced

1 cup (134 g) pitted green olives

¾ cup (124 g) raisins—this will bring a nice sweetness to the dish to even out the flavors well

3 cups (555 g) uncooked Basmati rice

¼ cup (4 g) chopped parsley, for serving

¼ cup (15 g) chopped cilantro, for serving

3 lbs (1.4 kg) boneless thick-cut pork chops

4 cloves garlic, minced

Zest of 1 lemon, divided

1 lemon, juiced

2 tbsp (30 ml) olive oil

1 tsp salt

2 tsp (5 g) pepper

3 tbsp (23 g) flour

Mashed potatoes or roasted cauliflower, for serving

BONELESS LEMON PEPPER PORK CHOPS

For years I avoided recipes that worked citrus into an entrée—especially lemon, as I felt it only belonged in lemonade and desserts. But I have since learned to appreciate the versatility of citrus, including it in many of my favorite savory comfort-food recipes. The combination of lemon and pepper in these pork chops is a perfect marriage of flavor. If you are like me, and ready to rethink lemons, I challenge you to give it a try!

1. Add the pork chops, garlic, half of the lemon zest, lemon juice, olive oil, salt and pepper to your 6-quart (6-L) slow cooker. Give it a quick mix, flipping the pork chops to coat in the oil and juice. Cover and cook on high for 4 hours or on low for 8 hours—the pork should reach an internal temperature of 155 to 160°F (68 to 71°C).

2. Remove the pork chops from your slow cooker and let them rest on a separate plate until the sauce is done. If cooking on low, turn your slow cooker to high, sprinkle the flour into the cooking liquid and whisk until it thickens to your desired consistency.

3. Top the pork chops with the remaining lemon zest. Serve with mashed potatoes or roasted cauliflower, along with the sauce.

2 lbs (908 g) boneless, skinless chicken thighs, cut into bite-sized pieces

1 tsp salt

¼ tsp pepper

1 large yellow onion, halved and thinly sliced lengthwise

2 cloves garlic, minced

3 tbsp (20 g) sweet paprika—not the smoked variety or this dish won't be edible!

5 tbsp (39 g) flour

1 (14.5-oz [411-g]) can low-sodium chicken broth

1 (14.5-oz [411-g]) can diced tomatoes

3 cups (555 g) uncooked Basmati rice

½ cup (120 ml) sour cream

Chopped parsley, for garnish

CHICKEN PAPRIKASH OVER RICE

Chicken Paprikash is a Hungarian dish named after its ample use of paprika. With a stunning color and a flavor to match, it's a fantastic recipe if you're looking to break a food rut. Many paprikash recipes call for searing the chicken and sautéing the vegetables first. I found those steps to be unnecessary, making this recipe that much easier!

1. Stir the chicken, salt, pepper, onion, garlic, paprika, flour, broth and tomatoes together in your 6-quart (6-L) slow cooker. Cover and cook on high for 4 hours or on low for 8 hours.

2. Turn off your slow cooker and allow the meat to rest for 20 minutes, uncovered. Meanwhile, cook the rice according to the package directions. Once the rice is cooked, stir the sour cream into your slow cooker and serve the paprikash over the rice with fresh chopped parsley.

SLOW-ROASTED PORK SHOULDER

There's nothing quite like a slow-cooked pork roast. This one is no exception! Fall-apart tender and juicy, it's a perfect dinner to be served with mashed potatoes. You're sure to have leftovers that can be made into many things like pulled pork, ragu, tacos or quesadillas.

2 large onions, sliced

1 tsp dried basil

1 tsp dried oregano

1 tsp salt

½ tsp pepper

1 tbsp (3 g) dried rosemary

3 lbs (1.4 kg) pork shoulder roast

1 cup (240 ml) chicken broth

2 tsp (6 g) minced garlic

1. Place the onions in your 6-quart (6-L) slow cooker. Combine the basil, oregano, salt, pepper and rosemary in a small bowl. Rub the pork roast with the seasoning blend.

2. Place the roast on top of the onions, pour in the broth and top with the garlic. Cover and cook on high for 6 hours or on low for 10 hours—the meat should pull apart easily with two forks. Save some of the juice to spoon over the pork for serving.

1 tbsp (14 g) butter

1 tbsp (15 ml) olive oil

1 medium onion, chopped

1 cup (70 g) diced mushrooms

Salt and pepper, to taste

3 cloves garlic, finely minced

1 lb (454 g) ground beef

4 tsp (20 ml) Worcestershire sauce

1 tsp garlic salt

1 tsp onion powder

1 tsp chili powder

1 tsp ground cumin

½ tsp paprika

3 tbsp (41 g) brown sugar

1 (14.5-oz [411-g]) can fire-roasted tomatoes, diced

1 (6-oz [170-g]) can tomato paste

1¼ cups (300 ml) water

¼ cup (60 ml) ketchup

6 pretzel buns, halved, for serving

6 slices provolone cheese, for serving

EXTRA SLOPPY SLOPPY JOES

Sloppy Joes don't have their name without reason. I call these Extra Sloppy as I believe you should go big or go home! In fact, I think the messiness makes these sandwiches even more delicious. Give them a try—just don't forget the extra napkins!

1. Heat the butter and oil over medium heat in a large skillet. Add the onion and sauté for 5 minutes, then add in the mushrooms and season with salt and pepper. Once the vegetables are tender, for about 5 more minutes, stir in the garlic and add the ground beef. Cook until the beef is no longer pink, for about 5 to 7 minutes.

2. Pour the beef mixture into your 6-quart (6-L) slow cooker. Stir in the Worcestershire sauce, garlic salt, onion powder, chili powder, cumin, paprika, sugar, tomatoes, tomato paste, water and ketchup. Cover and cook on high for 4 hours or on low for 8 hours. Serve on pretzel buns with a slice of cheese.

ITALIAN ORA (HOUR)

In Italy, there is an ingredient that is in every dish that is made. If you're like me, you're probably thinking garlic, but this ingredient is love. Love and passion are the essential ingredients every Italian mother and grandmother puts into everything they do. The amount of time you see them spend in the kitchen is really the evidence of that. With that thought in mind, naming this section Italian Ora—*ora* meaning hour in Italian—was to encourage us to slow down and take an hour to eat our dinner, at the kitchen table, conversing with family and bringing love back to the kitchen. Luckily, thanks to your slow cooker, you don't have to spend as much time cooking as the Italians do! And as they say in Italy, *godere* (enjoy)!

TOP 5

- *Meatball Marinara Submarine Sandwiches (page 52)*
- *Meaty Bolognese Sauce (page 56)*
- *Shredded Beef Ragu over Pappardelle Pasta (page 58)*
- *Mozzarella Stuffed Chicken Meatballs (page 62)*
- *Chicken Cacciatore with Tomato and Onion (page 65)*

MEATBALL MARINARA SUBMARINE SANDWICHES

Meatball subs are one of my favorites. A little messy to eat, I will admit, but there's something about that, that makes them even more fun to eat. Meatballs are actually very easy to make, so there's no reason to cut corners by using the premade stuff. Simmering them in this homemade marinara results in them being so tender they'll practically melt in your mouth!

1. Combine the garlic, oregano, basil, tomato puree and diced tomatoes in your 6-quart (6-L) slow cooker.

2. Combine the breadcrumbs, water, beef, egg, garlic, salt, pepper and oregano in a large bowl. Using your hands, carefully mix until just combined—overworking this will result in the meatballs becoming tough. Gently form the mixture into 12 meatballs and place into your slow cooker.

3. Cover and cook on high for 4 hours or on low for 8 hours. Serve the meatballs with sauce on rolls topped with mozzarella cheese. Garnish with Parmesan cheese.

SERVES 4

SAUCE

2 cloves garlic, minced

1 tbsp (3 g) dried oregano

3 tbsp (6 g) fresh basil

1 (28-oz [828-ml]) can tomato puree

1 (15-oz [425-g]) can diced tomatoes

MEATBALLS

1 cup (136 g) fresh breadcrumbs

⅓ cup (80 ml) water

1 lb (454 g) ground beef chuck

1 large egg, lightly beaten

1 clove garlic, minced

Salt and pepper, to taste

½ tsp dried oregano

4 French or Italian rolls, for serving—I estimate 3 meatballs per sub

4 slices mozzarella cheese

Grated Parmesan cheese, for garnish

3 lbs (1.4 kg) beef chuck roast

2 tsp (12 g) salt

¼ tsp pepper

2 tsp (2 g) dried oregano

1 tsp red pepper flakes

3 cloves garlic, minced

1 tbsp (8 g) Italian seasoning

1 bay leaf

1 (12-oz [340-g]) jar roasted red peppers, chopped

1 cup (240 ml) tomato juice

10 French rolls

10 slices provolone cheese

Pepperoncini peppers, for serving

QUICK ITALIAN BEEF SANDWICHES WITH PROVOLONE

Nothing beats a great sandwich! When looking for a fun and flavorful break from the routine, these Italian-flavored shredded beef sandwiches are a delicious and quick throw-together meal. Serving this on fresh-from-the-bakery French rolls makes this even better!

1. Season the beef with salt and pepper and transfer to your 6-quart (6-L) slow cooker. Add the oregano, pepper flakes, garlic, Italian seasoning, bay leaf, red peppers and tomato juice. Cover and cook on high for 4 hours or on low for 8 hours.

2. Remove the beef and shred using two forks, add the peppers from the slow cooker and serve on French rolls with cooking juices. Top with provolone cheese and pepperoncini peppers.

MEATY BOLOGNESE SAUCE

SERVES 8

Bolognese (commonly called spaghetti sauce) is traditionally cooked low and slow for hours. So, it makes sense that a slow cooker would do that job extremely well! Browning the meat and sautéing the aromatics first will help develop a deeper flavor that otherwise wouldn't be there by just throwing the ingredients into your slow cooker.

1. Heat the oil in a large stockpot or Dutch oven over medium-high heat. Sauté the onion, celery and carrot for 6 to 8 minutes until tender. Stir in the garlic and ground beef and cook until the beef is no longer pink, for about 5 to 7 minutes.

2. Stir in the tomato paste, salt, thyme, oregano, pepper, basil, nutmeg, milk and wine. Bring to a rapid simmer for 15 minutes, and then transfer the mixture to your 6-quart (6-L) slow cooker and pour in the chopped tomatoes and tomato sauce.

3. Cover and cook on low for 8 hours. Turn off the heat and allow the mixture to rest uncovered for 30 minutes prior to serving—a painful step because this sauce smells so good, but I promise it's worth the wait! Meanwhile, cook the pasta according to the package directions. Serve over pasta.

1 tbsp (15 ml) olive oil

1 medium yellow onion, finely chopped

2 ribs celery, finely chopped

1 medium carrot, finely chopped

2 cloves garlic, minced

2 lbs (908 g) ground beef

2 (6-oz [170-g]) cans tomato paste

2 tsp (6 g) kosher salt

½ tsp dried thyme

1 tbsp (3 g) dried oregano

½ tsp pepper

1 tbsp (2 g) dried basil

⅛ tsp ground nutmeg

1 cup (240 ml) whole milk

½ cup (120 ml) red wine

3 (14-oz [397-g]) cans chopped tomatoes, drained

2 (15-oz [425-g]) cans tomato sauce

1 lb (454 g) spaghetti noodles

SHREDDED BEEF RAGU OVER PAPPARDELLE PASTA

Ragu is an extremely versatile Italian dish. While my favorite way to serve this is over pasta, it's great on polenta, or even in a sandwich! This rich sauce will soon be a family favorite! It also freezes well for quick and easy future meals.

SERVES 8

1 medium onion, finely diced

1 carrot, shredded

1 rib celery, finely diced

3 cloves garlic, minced

1 tbsp (3 g) dried oregano

1½ tsp (2 g) dried thyme

3 lbs (1.4 kg) beef chuck roast, cut in two

Salt and pepper, to taste

1 (28-oz [794-g]) can crushed tomatoes

6 tbsp (90 ml) tomato paste

½ cup (120 ml) red wine

3 bay leaves

1 lb (454 g) pappardelle pasta

Grated Parmesan, for serving

1. Combine the onion, carrot, celery, garlic, oregano and thyme in your 6-quart (6-L) slow cooker. Season the beef generously on all sides with salt and pepper and place in your slow cooker. Pour in the tomatoes, tomato paste, red wine and bay leaves. Cover and cook on high for 4 hours or on low for 8 hours.

2. Remove the beef and the bay leaves. Using two forks, shred the beef and then return it to your slow cooker. Cook the pasta according to the package directions. Before draining the pasta, reserve 1 cup (240 ml) of the pasta water. Add the pasta and reserved water back into the pasta pot, add the ragu and stir—the ragu sauce will actually thicken from the pasta water; this is a technique used in Italy and will help the sauce stick to the noodles. You won't need a lot for it to do its job. Serve with grated Parmesan.

1 tbsp (15 ml) oil

1 lb (454 g) ground
Italian sausage

1 (26-oz [737-g]) can
tomato pasta sauce

1 medium yellow onion,
finely chopped

4 cloves garlic, diced

2 yellow bell peppers,
cut into ½-inch (1.3-cm)
pieces

2 red bell peppers, cut
into ½-inch (1.3-cm)
pieces

12 oz (340 g) penne
pasta

Shredded Parmesan
cheese, for topping

ITALIAN SAUSAGE PENNE PASTA

Two of my favorite things about Italian dinners are Italian sausage and pasta. Throw them together, and you have made me one happy (partially) Italian boy. It's the best of both worlds! Buy hot Italian sausage for a bit of an extra kick or sweet Italian sausage for a milder flavor. Either way, this will easily become a new family favorite!

1. Heat the oil in a large skillet over medium-high heat. Cook the sausage until it is no longer pink, for about 5 to 7 minutes; set aside.

2. Add half of the tomato sauce to your 6-quart (6-L) slow cooker. Add the onion, garlic, yellow and red bell peppers and sausage and top with the remaining sauce. Cover and cook on high for 4 hours or on low for 8 hours.

3. Cook the pasta according to the package directions. Once the sausage mixture is done, add the cooked pasta and stir to coat. Serve sprinkled with the Parmesan.

1 lb (454 g) ground chicken

1 large egg, beaten

½ cup (28 g) panko breadcrumbs— unseasoned regular breadcrumbs will work just fine

2 tsp (5 g) Italian seasoning

1 tbsp (9 g) minced garlic

½ cup (40 g) shredded Parmesan

1 cup (240 ml) marinara sauce

½ cup (56 g) shredded mozzarella

CHICKEN PARMESAN MEATLOAF

Meatloaf is a classic comfort food and for whatever reason, I'm always exploring new ways to jazz it up. Not that there's anything wrong with the original, because I do love it! Here we have a fun Italian twist on the comfort food staple, merging two of my favorites—chicken Parmesan and meatloaf!

1. Combine the chicken, egg, breadcrumbs, Italian seasoning, garlic and Parmesan in a large mixing bowl. Using your hands—and I really do recommend using your hands or you risk over-mixing and making the final dish tough—mix together until fully incorporated.

2. Shape the mixture into a round loaf and place it carefully into your 6-quart (6-L) slow cooker. Cover and cook on high for 3 hours or on low for 6 hours. Spoon the marinara sauce over the top and sprinkle with mozzarella cheese. Let the meatloaf rest for about 10 minutes before cutting and serving.

MOZZARELLA STUFFED CHICKEN MEATBALLS

Spaghetti and meatballs are a classic—using ground chicken to make these meatballs a bit leaner and stuffing them with fresh mozzarella makes this a satisfying meal your whole family will enjoy. Use whole-wheat pasta to give your meal a good fiber boost as well!

1. Stir together the tomatoes, onion, wine, tomato paste, garlic, basil, oregano and salt in your 6-quart (6-L) slow cooker. Combine the chicken, egg, Parmesan, breadcrumbs, basil, oregano, garlic powder and salt in a medium bowl—be sure not to over mix this, as it can make the meat tough.

2. Scoop out 1 tablespoon (15 g) of the meat mixture, form it into a disk, place a mozzarella piece in the center and wrap the meat around the cheese, rolling to form into a ball. Repeat with the remaining meat and cheese. Carefully place the meatballs into your slow cooker. Cover and cook on high for 3 hours or on low for 6 hours.

3. Cook the pasta according to the package directions. Serve over cooked pasta.

SERVES 4

SAUCE

1 (28-oz [794-g]) can crushed tomatoes

½ medium onion, grated

¼ cup (60 ml) dry red wine

2 tbsp (30 ml) tomato paste

2 cloves garlic, minced

½ tsp dried basil

½ tsp dried oregano

¼ tsp salt

MEATBALLS

1 lb (454 g) ground chicken

1 large egg, lightly beaten

½ cup (50 g) grated Parmesan cheese

½ cup (28 g) panko breadcrumbs—unseasoned regular breadcrumbs would work just fine

½ tsp dried basil

½ tsp dried oregano

½ tsp garlic powder

½ tsp salt

8 oz (227 g) fresh mozzarella, cut into roughly ½-inch (1.3-cm) cubes

16 oz (454 g) spaghetti, cooked, for serving

1 medium onion, thinly sliced

1 red bell pepper, thinly sliced

1 green bell pepper, thinly sliced

3 cloves garlic, sliced

¼ cup (60 ml) white wine

1 (28-oz [794-g]) can crushed tomatoes

2 sprigs fresh thyme, stems removed

1 bay leaf

8 boneless, skinless chicken thighs

Salt and pepper, to taste

Fresh parsley, for garnish

CHICKEN CACCIATORE WITH TOMATO AND ONION

Chicken Cacciatore is a classic Italian braised dish commonly containing onion, garlic and tomatoes. Braised recipes are perfect for the slow cooker because that is the very thing for which the slow cooker was designed! The word *cacciatore* actually means "hunter" in Italian and is typically made with chicken or rabbit. Although I'm not afraid to try this with rabbit, I would imagine you'd feel more comfortable with chicken!

1. Add the onion, red and green peppers, garlic, wine, tomatoes, thyme and bay leaf to your 6-quart (6-L) slow cooker.

2. Season the chicken with salt and pepper. Transfer the chicken to your slow cooker. Cover and cook on high for 4 hours or on low for 8 hours.

3. Remove the bay leaf and serve garnished with fresh parsley.

ITALIAN SAUSAGE SUBS WITH PEPPERS AND ONIONS

There is so much that can be done with Italian sausage, and the combination of mixing it with peppers and onions is iconic and delicious. Putting it on a hoagie and serving it up just like that is the perfect combination for a delicious sandwich.

1. Stir together the crushed tomatoes, oregano, pepper flakes, oil, onion, bell peppers, salt and pepper in your 6-quart (6-L) slow cooker. Lay the sausage in a single layer over the mixture. Cover and cook on high for 3 hours or on low for 6 hours.

2. Sprinkle in the fresh basil and serve the sausages on toasted hoagie rolls with onions and peppers.

SERVES 5

1 (28-oz [794-g]) can crushed tomatoes

1 tsp dried oregano

⅛ tsp red pepper flakes

1 tbsp (15 ml) oil

1 large onion, sliced

2 bell peppers, thinly sliced

Salt and pepper, to taste

1 lb (454 g) Italian sausage links

1 tbsp (3 g) fresh basil, thinly sliced

5 hoagie rolls, toasted

ASIAN AT HOME

As I began getting more interested in cooking, there was one type of cuisine that always daunted me—anything Asian. I thought cooking Asian cuisine was out of the question due to the methods and complexity. Cooking with a wok seemed totally impossible. Not to mention, it involves ingredients I had no experience with, which added to my fears. Then I started researching and realized it's not as scary as I had thought! Now this book is on slow cooking—can we really make Asian-style meals that taste like the real deal?! I emphatically say, YES! These dishes deliver on the flavor you're looking for—no wok required!

TOP 5

- *Easy Beef and Broccoli with Rice (page 70)*
- *Spicy Chicken Lo Mein (page 73)*
- *Pineapple Short Ribs with Brown Gravy (page 80)*
- *Sticky Pork Sliders with Fresh Slaw (page 83)*
- *Pineapple Sweet and Sour Chicken (page 87)*

EASY BEEF AND BROCCOLI WITH RICE

When it comes to Asian cuisine, it doesn't get any more straightforward than beef and broccoli. This sweet and savory dish is perfect served over rice and looks as delicious as it tastes. Even picky eaters will enjoy this one!

1. Stir together the soy sauce, oyster sauce, sugar, oil, ginger, garlic and vinegar in a small bowl.

2. Add the onions and cubed steak to your 6-quart (6-L) slow cooker. Pour the sauce mixture over the top. Cover and cook on high for 4 hours or on low for 8 hours.

3. Prepare the rice according to package directions. Stir the cornstarch mixture and the broccoli into your slow cooker. If cooking on low, turn your slow cooker to high, and cook for 30 more minutes—the sauce will thicken and the broccoli will still have a bit of a crunch. Serve over rice.

SERVES 4

¼ cup (60 ml) soy sauce

3 tbsp (45 ml) oyster sauce

1 tbsp (14 g) brown sugar

1 tsp toasted sesame oil

1 tsp ground ginger

4 cloves garlic, sliced

1 tbsp (15 ml) Chinese rice wine vinegar

2 medium onions, finely diced

1 lb (454 g) flank steak or sirloin, cut into 1-inch (2.5-cm) cubes

2 cups (370 g) uncooked Basmati rice

1 tbsp (8 g) cornstarch, mixed with 1 tbsp (15 ml) water

1 head broccoli florets

SAUCE

⅔ cup (160 ml) low-sodium soy sauce

3 cloves garlic, minced

3 tbsp (38 g) sugar

2 tbsp (30 ml) oyster sauce

2 tsp (10 ml) sesame oil

2 tsp (4 g) ground ginger

2 tsp (10 ml) Sriracha chili sauce, or more to taste

CHICKEN LO MEIN

2 lbs (908 g) boneless, skinless chicken thighs

1 lb (454 g) spaghetti noodles or Chinese egg noodles

1 cup (63 g) snow peas, trimmed

1 red bell pepper, thinly sliced

2 carrots, thinly sliced

2 ribs celery, diagonally sliced

1 (5-oz [142-g]) can sliced water chestnuts

3 cups (90 g) baby spinach

SPICY CHICKEN LO MEIN

Lo Mein is a takeout classic! It's loaded with crunchy vegetables and has a savory sauce with a small amount of heat. All the healthy vegetables make this dish one of my favorites. Any time you can get a dish that is both nutritious and delicious, it is a winner for me!

1. Stir together the soy sauce, garlic, sugar, oyster sauce, oil, ginger and Sriracha in a medium bowl.

2. Add the chicken to your 6-quart (6-L) slow cooker. Pour the soy sauce mixture over the chicken, cover and cook on high for 4 hours or on low for 8 hours.

3. Prepare the pasta according to package directions. Remove the chicken from your slow cooker, shred it using two forks and set aside. If cooking on low, turn your slow cooker to high, add the peas, pepper, carrots, celery and water chestnuts. Cover and cook for 20 more minutes—this will cook the vegetables just enough to have a bit of a crunch. Before serving, stir in the cooked noodles, chicken and spinach; serve immediately.

TANGY ORANGE CHINESE CHICKEN

My favorite dish when ordering Chinese takeout is orange chicken, and this version will make you believe you just ordered from the restaurant. Making it yourself gives you the experience without the delivery fee.

1. Add the chicken to your 6-quart (6-L) slow cooker, sprinkle in the flour and stir to coat. Stir in the orange marmalade, water, sugar, soy sauce, ginger, oil, vinegar, garlic, pepper flakes and onion. Cover and cook on high for 4 hours or on low for 8 hours.

2. Prepare the rice according to the package directions. Serve over rice, topped with green onion.

SERVES 4

8 boneless, skinless chicken thighs

3 tbsp (23 g) flour

⅓ cup (80 ml) orange marmalade

¼ cup (60 ml) water

2 tbsp (28 g) brown sugar

2 tbsp (30 ml) soy sauce

1 tbsp (6 g) freshly grated ginger

1 tsp toasted sesame oil

1 tbsp (15 ml) Chinese rice wine vinegar

1 tsp minced garlic

½ tsp crushed red pepper flakes

¼ cup (25 g) chopped green onion, plus more for serving

2 cups (370 g) uncooked Basmati rice

1 cup (240 ml) unsweetened coconut milk—about half of a can

⅓ cup (85 g) creamy peanut butter

2 tbsp (30 ml) low-sodium soy sauce

2 tbsp (30 ml) honey

1 tbsp (15 ml) Chinese rice wine vinegar

1 tbsp (6 g) freshly grated ginger

3 cloves garlic, minced

3 boneless, skinless chicken breasts, cut into 1-inch (2.5-cm) chunks

3 cups (555 g) uncooked Basmati rice

1 tbsp (15 ml) lime juice

¼ cup (32 g) cornstarch mixed with ¼ cup (60 ml) water

TOPPINGS

Lime wedges

Chopped peanuts

Cilantro

Green onions

THAI PEANUT CHICKEN AND RICE

Peanut butter lovers rejoice! If you're familiar with Thai cuisine, you know there's no shortage of flavor, and this dish is no exception. While garnishes are considered optional in American cuisines, that is not the case here. The garnishes offer texture, additional flavor and a fresh hit that cuts through the richness, all while adding so much more to this dish. You won't regret adding them!

1. Stir together the milk, peanut butter, soy sauce, honey, vinegar, ginger and garlic in your 6-quart (6-L) slow cooker. Add in the chicken, cover and cook on high for 3 hours or on low for 6 hours.

2. Prepare the rice according to package directions. Stir the lime juice and the cornstarch mixture into your slow cooker, and cook for 20 more minutes. If cooking on low, turn your slow cooker to high and stir until the sauce has thickened. Serve over rice with a lime wedge on the side and topped with chopped peanuts, cilantro and green onions.

PORK TENDERLOIN FAUX FRY

Since stir-frying is actually a cooking technique, it didn't feel right using the term here. Hence, a "faux fry" that has all your favorite ingredients from a stir-fry, but made much easier and healthier!

SERVES 6

2 tbsp (30 ml) olive oil

2 lbs (908 g) pork tenderloin, cut into ½-inch (1.3-cm) medallions

½ cup (120 ml) teriyaki sauce

1 cup (240 ml) chicken broth

¼ cup (55 g) brown sugar

4 cloves garlic, minced

1 large onion, sliced

¼ tsp black pepper

3 cups (555 g) uncooked Basmati rice

2 red bell peppers, sliced

1. Heat the oil in a large skillet over medium-high heat. Brown the tenderloin medallions on both sides, for about 3 minutes per side. Meanwhile, mix together the teriyaki sauce, broth, sugar, garlic, onion and black pepper in a medium bowl.

2. Pour half of the sauce on the bottom of your 6-quart (6-L) slow cooker, add the pork medallions and cover with the remaining sauce mixture. Cover and cook on high for 4 hours or on low for 8 hours.

3. Prepare the rice according to package directions. If cooking on low, turn your slow cooker to high, add the sliced peppers and cook for 20 more minutes—the peppers will still have a bit of a crunch. Serve over rice with the sauce.

1½ lbs (681 g) pork tenderloin

½ cup (120 ml) pineapple juice, from canned pineapple below

½ cup (120 ml) hoisin sauce

2 tsp (4 g) ground ginger

1 tbsp (15 ml) soy sauce

2 tsp (10 ml) Dijon mustard

3 cloves garlic, minced

1 (14.5-oz [411-g]) can pineapple rings, reserve juice

2 cups (370 g) uncooked rice

1 lb (454 g) fresh snow peas, trimmed

PORK TENDERLOIN WITH PINEAPPLE-GINGER GLAZE

There's nothing like slow-cooking to bring out the complexity in flavors like pineapple and ginger. This Asian-inspired pork tenderloin contains the perfect combination of sweet and savory, and the snow peas add a wonderful crunchy texture to round out this meal.

1. Place the pork tenderloin into your 6-quart (6-L) slow cooker. Remove the pineapple juice from the can and stir in a small bowl with the hoisin sauce, ginger, soy sauce, mustard and garlic. Pour the mixture over the tenderloin, turning to coat. Place the pineapple rings on the top, cover and cook on low for 4 hours.

2. Prepare the rice according to package directions. Add the snow peas to your slow cooker and cook for 20 more minutes. Serve over rice with the cooking liquid and snow peas.

PINEAPPLE SHORT RIBS WITH BROWN GRAVY

SERVES 6

3 lbs (1.4 kg) lean bone-in beef short ribs

1 (16-oz [454-g]) can pineapple chunks, reserve juice

¼ cup (60 ml) water

¼ cup (60 ml) soy sauce

1½ tsp (3 g) ground ginger

⅓ cup (42 g) flour

¼ cup (60 ml) honey

1 tbsp (14 g) brown sugar

This is actually an old family recipe that came from my grandmother, who made it quite often. While this recipe certainly isn't an authentic Asian recipe, it definitely is delicious. It is full of flavor and makes an incredible brown gravy. Serve this on rice or even over mashed potatoes.

1. Add the short ribs and pineapple chunks to your 6-quart (6-L) slow cooker. Stir the water, soy sauce, ginger, flour, reserved pineapple juice, honey and sugar together in a medium bowl.

2. Pour the sauce mixture over the short ribs and pineapple. Cover and cook on high for 4 hours or on low for 8 hours. Serve the short ribs and pineapple with the brown gravy.

2 lbs (908 g) pork shoulder roast, cut into 1- to 2-inch (2.5–5-cm) pieces

1 cup (240 ml) chicken broth

2-inch (5-cm) piece fresh ginger, grated

3 cloves garlic, sliced

2 tbsp (30 ml) dry sherry

1 red chili, thinly sliced or minced

3 tbsp (45 ml) honey

2 tbsp (28 g) brown sugar

¼ cup (60 ml) soy sauce

16 prepared bao buns

SLAW

1 cup (122 g) thinly sliced carrots

1 cup (105 g) sliced cucumbers

¼ cup (25 g) sliced green onions

¼ cup (4 g) chopped cilantro

1 tbsp (15 ml) rice wine vinegar

STICKY PORK SLIDERS WITH FRESH SLAW

When I think of Asian comfort food, I think of these pork sliders. These are traditionally made with pork belly, but I substituted a leaner cut of pork. These are absolutely delicious and full of sweet and savory flavors! The richness of this pork is cut with a hit of fresh slaw to top them off. These make great entrées, or serve them up as appetizers!

1. Add the pork to your 6-quart (6-L) slow cooker. Stir the broth, ginger, garlic, sherry, chili, honey, sugar and soy sauce together in a medium bowl. Pour the mixture over the pork and stir. Cover and cook on high for 4 hours or on low for 8 hours. Meanwhile, combine the carrot, cucumber, green onion, cilantro and vinegar in a small bowl, cover and refrigerate.

2. Remove the pork from the slow cooker. Transfer the cooking liquid to a saucepan, bring the mixture to a boil and reduce to about 1 cup (240 ml)—I know this sounds a bit tedious, but we are saving on ingredients by just repurposing the cooking liquid versus making another sauce. While the liquid boils, shred the meat using two forks. Return the shredded pork to the slow cooker, pour in the reduced liquid and stir to combine.

3. Serve the pork in the prepared bao buns and top with the prepared slaw.

PEPPER STEAK WITH RICE

If you have had pepper steak before, this recipe needs no introduction. If you haven't, this dish is a staple served at just about any Chinese takeout restaurant. While this recipe may not be exactly authentic—cooking it in a slow cooker definitely is not—it's still incredibly tasty!

1. Stir the broth, soy sauce, ginger, garlic and sugar together in a medium bowl.

2. Add the onion and sirloin to your 6-quart (6-L) slow cooker. Pour over the broth mixture, cover and cook on high for 4 hours or on low for 8 hours.

3. Prepare the rice according to package directions. If cooking on low, turn your slow cooker to high, stir in the cornstarch mixture, add the sliced peppers and cook for 20 more minutes—the sauce will thicken and the peppers will still have a bit of a crunch. Serve over rice with the sauce.

SERVES 6

3 cups (720 ml) beef broth

3 tbsp (45 ml) soy sauce

1 tsp finely chopped ginger root or ½ tsp ground ginger

2 cloves garlic, minced

1 tbsp (13 g) sugar, optional

1 medium onion, sliced

1½ lbs (681 g) sirloin steak, sliced thinly across the grain—using slightly frozen sirloin will make slicing much easier

3 cups (555 g) uncooked Basmati rice

¼ cup (32 g) cornstarch, mixed with ¼ cup (60 ml) water

1 large green bell pepper, sliced

1 large red bell pepper, sliced

½ cup (110 g) light brown sugar

¼ cup (60 ml) Chinese rice wine vinegar

¼ cup (60 ml) ketchup

1 tsp grated fresh ginger, or ½ tsp ground ginger

½ cup (120 ml) chicken stock

½ cup (120 ml) pineapple juice, from canned pineapple below

1½ lbs (681 g) boneless, skinless chicken thighs, cut into 1-inch (2.5-cm) cubes

Salt and pepper, to taste

2 cups (370 g) uncooked Basmati rice

2 tbsp (16 g) cornstarch, mixed with 2 tbsp (30 ml) water

1 red bell pepper, chopped

½ lb (227 g) snow peas

3 green onions, cut into 1-inch (2.5-cm) pieces

1 cup (240 ml) canned pineapple chunks, reserve juice

PINEAPPLE SWEET AND SOUR CHICKEN

This sweet and sour chicken is a perfect weeknight meal. Save yourself time by doing the first two steps in the morning before work. That way, when you get home, it's as simple as preparing the rice and veggies, and dinner is done!

1. Stir the sugar, vinegar, ketchup, ginger, stock and juice together in a medium bowl.

2. Add the chicken to your 6-quart (6-L) slow cooker and season with salt and pepper. Pour the sauce mixture over the chicken, cover and cook on high for 4 hours or on low for 8 hours.

3. Prepare the rice according to package directions. If cooking on low, turn your slow cooker to high, stir in the cornstarch mixture and add the pepper, peas, onions and pineapple. Cover and cook for 20 more minutes—this will cook the vegetables just enough to still have a bit of a crunch. Serve over rice with the sauce.

SOUTH OF THE BORDER

When I think of south-of-the-border foods, my mind goes right to my favorite Mexican and Tex-Mex style restaurants. All of the spice and culture that can be exhibited through this food makes this section one you are sure to enjoy. Mexican food always packs a punch in the flavor department. Making these dishes in your slow cooker allows you to create that flavor punch right in your very own kitchen. No travel necessary for that Mexican flair.

TOP 5

- *Sirloin Fajitas with Peppers and Onions (page 90)*
- *Bold Mexican Shredded Beef (page 93)*
- *Simple Shredded Pork Carnitas (page 96)*
- *Creamy Chicken Tortilla Soup (page 99)*
- *Pozole—New Mexican–Style Soup (page 100)*

SIRLOIN FAJITAS WITH PEPPERS AND ONIONS

If you say Tex-Mex, the first thing I think of is fajitas! Served on a sizzling plate, the visual presentation and tempting aroma make them pretty hard to pass up! This recipe is just as good as any restaurant version, but made right at home. (Minus the sizzling plate of course!)

1. Stir the sirloin, oil, juice, garlic, cumin, seasoning salt and chili powder together in your 6-quart (6-L) slow cooker. Cover and cook on high for 3 hours or on low for 6 hours.

2. If cooking on low, turn your slow cooker to high, add the green pepper and onion, cover and cook for 1 more hour.

3. Serve the fajitas in the warmed tortillas with toppings.

SERVES 8

2 lbs (908 g) boneless sirloin, cut into thin strips

2 tbsp (30 ml) oil

2 tbsp (30 ml) lime juice

2 cloves garlic, minced

1 tsp ground cumin

2 tsp (10 g) seasoning salt (I use Lawry's)

1 tsp chili powder

1 green bell pepper, thinly sliced

1 onion, thinly sliced

8–12 flour tortillas, warmed

TOPPINGS

Shredded cheese

Salsa

Guacamole

Sour cream

Shredded lettuce

Chopped tomato

Chopped onion

1 large onion, diced

3 lbs (1.4 kg) beef chuck roast

1 cup (240 ml) beef broth

4 oz (120 ml) Mexican-style tomato sauce, mild—if you prefer spicy, hot sauce will bring the heat

2 cloves garlic, minced

1 tsp ground cumin

1 tbsp (8 g) chili powder

1½ tsp (9 g) salt

Tortilla shells, flour or corn, for serving

TOPPINGS

Chopped cilantro

Sour cream

Cotija cheese, or other cheese

Diced onion

Lime wedges

BOLD MEXICAN SHREDDED BEEF

This shredded beef with its south-of-the-border flavor is the perfect filling for tacos and quesadillas or for a piled-high plate of nachos. You can make this dish go even further by adding a variety of toppings and serving it in mini tortillas to make this a great appetizer!

1. Place the onion in your 6-quart (6-L) slow cooker and set the roast on top. Add the broth, sauce, garlic, cumin, chili powder and salt, cover and cook on high for 4 hours or on low for 8 hours.

2. Using two forks, carefully shred the beef in the liquid. Serve in tortillas topped with cilantro, sour cream, Cotija cheese and diced onion with lime wedges on the side.

SPICY CHICKEN ENCHILADA SOUP

Taking something as amazing as chicken enchiladas and saying you're going to tinker with the recipe would normally make my jaw drop, but after trying my first enchilada soup, I knew I must include one in this book! You'll save tons of time and possibly have a new favorite, too.

1. Stir the chicken, onion, garlic, chili powder, cumin, oregano, broth, tomato sauce, tomatoes, beans and corn together in your 6-quart (6-L) slow cooker. Cover and cook on high for 4 hours or on low for 8 hours.

2. Serve in bowls topped with tortilla strips, sour cream, cilantro, avocado and cheese.

1 lb (454 g) boneless, skinless chicken thighs, cut into 1-inch (2.5-cm) pieces

1 small onion, chopped

3 cloves garlic, minced

2 tsp (5 g) chili powder

1 tsp ground cumin

1 tsp dried oregano

3 cups (720 ml) chicken broth

8 oz (240 ml) hot tomato sauce

1 (14.5-oz [411-g]) can diced tomatoes

1 (14.5-oz [411-g]) can black beans

1 lb (454 g) corn—fresh, frozen or canned is fine here

TOPPINGS

Tortilla strips

Sour cream

Chopped cilantro

Diced avocado

Shredded cheese

2 lbs (908 g) boneless, skinless chicken thighs

⅓ cup (42 g) flour

4 cloves garlic, sliced

½ cup (120 ml) prepared salsa, reserve the rest for serving

2 tbsp (30 g) chopped canned chipotle chilies in adobo

1 tbsp (8 g) chili powder

1 tsp coarse salt

1 tsp ground pepper

8 hard corn taco shells

TOPPINGS

Cilantro

Shredded cheese

Lime wedges

Sour cream

AMAZING SHREDDED CHICKEN TACOS

Tacos are one my favorite foods, and shredded chicken with all of the spice you can pair with it makes for one good taco—or maybe even eight of them! The chicken cooks right in the spices and absorbs all of it to result in a taco that will make you salivate.

1. Combine the chicken, flour, garlic, salsa, chilies, chili powder, salt and pepper in your 6-quart (6-L) slow cooker. Cover and cook on high for 4 hours or on low for 8 hours.

2. Transfer the chicken to a plate and use two forks to shred; add the chicken back in the slow cooker. Serve in taco shells with toppings, if desired.

*See photo on page 88.

SIMPLE SHREDDED PORK CARNITAS

I love some good shredded pork paired with excellent spices and thrown into a warmed tortilla with some avocado and sour cream—that's what I call the perfect carnitas. Don't just take my word for it; give it a try! You'll be amazed at how simple and delicious this meal can be. I promise you won't regret it.

1. Combine the pork, garlic, cilantro, onion, oregano, broth, salt and pepper in your 6-quart (6-L) slow cooker. Cover and cook on high for 3 hours or on low for 6 hours.

2. Transfer the pork to a plate, and shred using two forks. Add the meat back to your slow cooker. Serve in tortillas, topped with more cilantro, avocado, lime, sour cream and cheese.

SERVES 6

2 lbs (908 g) boneless pork shoulder

4 cloves garlic, minced

1 tbsp (1 g) minced fresh cilantro, plus more for serving

1 large onion, chopped

1½ tsp (2 g) dried oregano

1 (14.5-oz [411-g]) can low-sodium chicken broth

Salt and pepper, to taste

12 corn or flour tortillas, toasted or warmed

TOPPINGS

Diced avocado

Lime wedges

Sour cream

Shredded cheese

1 lb (454 g) boneless, skinless chicken thighs

2 (14.5-oz [411-g]) cans Mexican stewed tomatoes and chilies—I use RO*TEL

2 (14.5-oz [411-g]) cans chicken broth

1 (16-oz [454-g]) can refried beans

1 lb (454 g) corn— fresh, frozen or canned is fine here

TOPPINGS

Shredded Monterey Jack cheese

Corn tortilla strips

2 tsp (1 g) fresh cilantro, chopped

CREAMY CHICKEN TORTILLA SOUP

Normally, when you think of a creamy soup, you assume there will be some sort of dairy, but this recipe changes that assumption! It's thickened with refried beans and tastes incredible, not to mention the beans add another dose of protein!

1. Add the chicken, stewed tomatoes and chilies, broth, beans and corn to your 6-quart (6-L) slow cooker. Cover and cook on high for 4 hours or on low for 8 hours.

2. Serve with cheese, tortilla strips and cilantro.

POZOLE— NEW MEXICAN— STYLE SOUP

I have family that lives in New Mexico. When I told my cousin I was writing a slow cooker book, she insisted I try out her recipe for *pozole*. It's a pork stew with a little kick and a great texture from the hominy. If you're looking to sample something new and with a bit of heat, this is a must try!

1. Stir the cumin, paprika, oregano, salt and pepper together in a large bowl. Add the cubed pork and toss. Transfer the meat and any remaining spices to your 6-quart (6-L) slow cooker. Add the onion, broth, tomatoes, hominy and chili sauce. Cover and cook on high for 4 hours or on low for 8 hours.

2. Before serving, stir in the lime juice and season to taste with salt. Serve with lime wedges.

SERVES 6

1 tsp ground cumin

½ tsp smoked paprika

1 tsp dried oregano

1½ tsp (9 g) salt, plus more for serving

1 tsp pepper

2 lbs (908 g) boneless pork shoulder, cut into ½-inch (1.3-cm) cubes

1 onion, chopped

3 cups (720 ml) chicken broth

1 (15.5-oz [439-g]) can diced tomatoes

1 (15-oz [425-g]) can hominy, drained

1 (8-oz [227-g]) can red chili sauce—not enchilada sauce

2 tbsp (30 ml) lime juice

Lime wedges, for serving

BY THE SPOONFUL

No slow cooker cookbook would be complete without a section of delicious soups! Whether it was used to alleviate a cold or warm up after a day in the snow, soup plays a big role in my childhood memories. This chapter focuses on soups as they should be made, in large batches! Soup is a warm comfort that makes any dish better as a side but is just as good (if not better) as the entrée! I've included some everyday favorites along with some that may surprise but will no doubt satisfy. It's time to rethink soup!

TOP 5

- *Easy Shredded Chicken and Dumplings (page 104)*
- *Coney Island–Style Chili (page 113)*
- *Sweet and Creamy Corn Chowder (page 114)*
- *Savory Beef and Barley Stew (page 118)*
- *Sausage and Shrimp Cajun Stew (page 125)*

EASY SHREDDED CHICKEN AND DUMPLINGS

While many variations exist, this recipe is inspired by the American southern classic. The slow-cooked, pull-apart chicken, the creamy broth and tender biscuit-style dumplings make this one a hit! Everyone I know, including myself, loves a hot bowl of chicken and dumplings!

1. Add the onion, carrots, celery, garlic, water, broth, chicken, bay leaf, Old Bay seasoning, salt and pepper to your 6-quart (6-L) slow cooker. Cover and cook on high for 4 hours or on low for 8 hours.

2. Remove the bay leaf and cooked chicken. Using two forks, shred the chicken—this sounds more laborious than it is. The chicken is so tender it's practically effortless. Stir the flour mixture and shredded chicken into your slow cooker.

3. Combine the flour, baking powder and salt in a medium bowl. Cut in the butter and stir in the milk. Using a measuring cup, drop scoops of the dough into the soup mixture. If cooking on low, turn your slow cooker to high, cover and continue to cook for 1 more hour.

SERVES 6

1 large onion, finely diced

2 cups (244 g) sliced carrots

2 cups (202 g) sliced celery

2 cloves garlic, minced

2 cups (480 ml) water

4 cups (960 ml) chicken broth

2 lbs (908 g) boneless, skinless chicken thighs

1 dried bay leaf

1 tsp Old Bay or poultry seasoning

Salt and pepper, to taste

½ cup (64 g) flour, mixed with ½ cup (120 ml) water

DUMPLINGS

1 cup (125 g) flour

1 tsp baking powder

½ tsp salt

2 tbsp (28 g) butter

½ cup (120 ml) milk

2 lbs (908 g) ground
beef

1 green bell pepper,
diced

1 medium onion, diced

2 (14-oz [397-g]) cans
kidney beans, drained

2 (14-oz [397-g]) cans
pinto beans, drained

1 (14-oz [397-g]) can
crushed tomatoes

1 (6-oz [177-ml]) can
tomato paste

1 (24-oz [709-ml]) can
tomato juice

1 tbsp (8 g) chili
powder

1 tsp salt

½ tsp pepper

HEARTY BEEF AND BEAN CHILI

My family makes some of the heartiest chilies I have ever had. This recipe is so full of meat, beans and flavor, you just can't go wrong. Making it in a slow cooker develops the flavors even further, giving this chili a warm complexity and incredible taste! I had to include it in this book for you to enjoy.

1. Heat a large skillet over medium-high heat. Add in the ground beef, cooking until no longer pink, for about 5 to 7 minutes.

2. Add the beef, bell pepper, onion, kidney beans, pinto beans, tomatoes, tomato paste, tomato juice, chili powder, salt and pepper to your 6-quart (6-L) slow cooker and stir. Cover and cook on high for 4 hours or on low for 8 hours.

BEEFY STUFFED CABBAGE SOUP

This easy throw-together soup is a fun twist on stuffed cabbage! It tastes just like the traditional stuffed cabbage, but in soup form, and saves you time in the kitchen. Next time, skip the burgers and get creative with your ground beef.

1. Heat a large skillet over medium-high heat. Add the beef and cook until no longer pink, for about 5 to 7 minutes. Combine the beef, onion, garlic, bell peppers, cabbage, salt, pepper, paprika, pepper flakes, Worcestershire sauce, bay leaf, broth, juice and water together in your 6-quart (6-L) slow cooker. Cover and cook on high for 4 hours or on low for 8 hours.

2. If cooking on low, turn your slow cooker to high, stir in the rice, cover and continue to cook for 30 more minutes. Remove the bay leaf before serving.

SERVES 6

1 lb (454 g) ground beef

1 medium onion, chopped

2 cloves garlic, minced

2 red bell peppers, chopped

1 small cabbage, shredded—shredded bagged cabbage used for coleslaw works here too

1 tsp salt

½ tsp pepper

1 tsp paprika

¼ tsp crushed red pepper flakes

1 tbsp (15 ml) Worcestershire sauce

1 bay leaf

4 cups (960 ml) beef broth

2½ cups (600 ml) tomato juice

3 cups (720 ml) water

1 cup (190 g) uncooked brown rice

CREAMY ITALIAN SAUSAGE, BEAN AND KALE SOUP

Protein-packed, nutritious and delicious, this soup can stand alone . . . it has all the makings of a main course and couldn't be easier to prepare!

1 tbsp (15 ml) olive oil

1 lb (454 g) ground Italian sausage

2 cloves garlic, minced

½ tsp onion powder

4 cups (960 ml) chicken broth

1 cup (240 ml) water

4 (14-oz [397-g]) cans navy beans, drained

Salt and pepper, to taste

½ cup (120 ml) half-and-half

4 cups (268 g) kale, stems removed, finely chopped or shredded

Crusty bread, for serving

1. Heat the oil in a large skillet over medium-high heat. Add the sausage and cook until no longer pink, for about 5 to 7 minutes. Stir together the sausage, garlic, onion powder, broth, water, beans, salt and pepper in your 6-quart (6-L) slow cooker. Cover and cook on high for 3 hours or on low for 6 hours.

2. A half hour before cooking time is up, stir in the half-and-half and the kale, cover and continue to cook for the remaining time. Serve with bread on the side.

1 carrot, finely minced

1 rib celery, finely minced

1 medium onion, finely minced

2 cloves garlic, finely minced

7 (15.5-oz [439-g]) cans Great Northern beans, rinsed and drained

½ to 1 tsp crushed red pepper flakes, optional

1 ham shank—cubed ham would work here as well but a shank offers a much richer flavor

1½ quarts (1.4 L) chicken broth

Salt and pepper, to taste

RICH BEAN AND HAM SOUP

Bean soups are protein-packed and very budget friendly. Add just a few other ingredients and they come together to make a delicious soup that's perfect in the winter or really any chilly evening. This soup has been a staple in my household for quite some time now, and I'm sure it will soon become one for you too!

1. Add the carrot, celery, onion, garlic and beans to your 6-quart (6-L) slow cooker—add the pepper flakes to give a little more of a kick to your soup, but don't worry, you can just omit them if heat isn't your thing. Place the ham shank into the slow cooker and pour in the chicken broth. Cover and cook on high for 5 hours or on low for 10 hours.

2. Remove the ham shank, slice off the meat and stir the meat back into the soup. Season to taste and serve.

1 lb (454 g) ground beef

2 tbsp (14 g) onion powder

1 tsp garlic powder

1 tsp chili powder

1 tsp paprika

½ tsp ground cumin

2 tsp (10 g) seasoning salt (I use Lawry's)

1 (14-oz [414-ml]) can tomato puree

1 cup (240 ml) water

1 tbsp (15 ml) prepared yellow mustard

OPTIONAL—BUT RECOMMENDED

Hot dogs

Hot dog buns

Shredded cheese

Diced onions

Mustard

CONEY ISLAND–STYLE CHILI

It doesn't matter how long it has been since you have had Coney Island–style chili; one taste of this slow-cooked version, and you will instantly remember that time! Having this recipe on hand will save you a trip to the diner, but be sure you have all the toppings or it just won't be the same!

1. Heat a large skillet over medium-high heat. Add the ground beef and cook until no longer pink, for about 5 to 7 minutes. Stir in the onion powder, garlic powder, chili powder, paprika, cumin and seasoning salt until well combined. Add the seasoned meat, tomato puree and water to your 6-quart (6-L) slow cooker and stir. Cover and cook on high for 3 hours or on low for 6 hours.

2. Before serving, stir in the mustard and serve in a bowl or over hot dogs— the classic Coney dog can also be served with shredded cheese, diced onions, mustard or a combination of all three.

SWEET AND CREAMY CORN CHOWDER

SERVES 6

1 lb (454 g) small potatoes, diced into ½-inch (1.3-cm) pieces

2 (16-oz [454-g]) packages frozen corn

1 medium onion, finely diced

1 rib celery, finely diced

2 cloves garlic, minced

6 cups (1.4 L) chicken broth

1 tsp dried thyme

3 tbsp (24 g) cornstarch

½ cup (120 ml) heavy cream

2 tbsp (28 g) butter

When I think of chowders, I think of filling, hunger-satisfying soups. They are something I love when coming in from the cold or rain. This recipe may not have any meat, but it is no less satisfying. There's never a bad time to make up a batch of this delicious soup.

1. Combine the potatoes, corn, onion, celery, garlic, broth and thyme in your 6-quart (6-L) slow cooker. Cover and cook on high for 4 hours or on low for 8 hours.

2. Combine the cornstarch and the heavy cream in a small bowl and stir until smooth. Stir the mixture and the butter into the soup and let stand for 15 minutes before serving.

1½ cups (183 g) sliced carrots

1½ cups (152 g) sliced celery

1 small onion, diced

2 cloves garlic, minced

8 boneless, skinless chicken thighs

2 bay leaves

5 tsp (30 g) salt

1 tsp pepper

1 tsp thyme

1 tsp rosemary

12 cups (2.9 L) chicken broth

1 (12-oz [340-g]) package egg noodles

CLASSIC SHREDDED CHICKEN NOODLE SOUP

There's nothing like a bowl of chicken noodle soup on a cold winter day, or any day for that matter. This recipe is delicious and incredibly simple to make. Letting it cook all day delivers the best possible flavors.

1. Add the carrots, celery, onion, garlic, chicken, bay leaves, salt, pepper, thyme, rosemary and broth to your 6-quart (6-L) slow cooker. Cover and cook on high for 4 hours or on low for 8 hours.

2. Remove the chicken from your slow cooker and shred it using two forks—this sounds more laborious than it is. The chicken is so tender it's practically effortless. Add the noodles and the shredded chicken to your slow cooker. If cooking on low, turn your slow cooker to high, cover and continue to cook for 20 more minutes.

SAVORY BEEF AND BARLEY STEW

A family favorite, this savory beef and barley stew is the perfect recipe for the slow cooker. It's a wholesome and filling dish that you can make for a large crowd. What I love about this meal is it stands alone as a well-rounded dinner.

1. Add the meat, onion, carrots, celery, mushrooms, bay leaf, broth, onion powder, thyme, parsley, Old Bay seasoning, soy sauce, Worcestershire sauce, salt and pepper to your 6-quart (6-L) slow cooker and stir. Cover and cook on high for 4 hours or on low for 8 hours.

2. If cooking on low, turn your slow cooker to high, stir in the barley, cover and continue to cook for 30 more minutes. Remove the bay leaf before serving.

SERVES 8

2 lbs (908 g) beef stew meat, cut into ½-inch (1.3-cm) cubes

1 medium onion, diced

3 carrots, diced

2 ribs celery, sliced

8 oz (227 g) mini bella mushrooms, sliced

1 bay leaf

8 cups (1.9 L) beef broth

1 tsp onion powder

½ tsp thyme

1 tbsp (2 g) dried parsley

1 tsp Old Bay seasoning

1 tbsp (15 ml) soy sauce

2 tsp (10 ml) Worcestershire sauce

Salt and pepper, to taste

2 cups (400 g) quick pearl barley

2 lbs (908 g) beef stew meat, cut into ½-inch (1.3-cm) cubes

1 tsp salt

½ tsp pepper

1 lb (454 g) frozen pearl onions

1 large white onion, diced

3 ribs celery, sliced

3 large carrots, sliced

3 lbs (1.4 kg) red potatoes, quartered

½ lb (227 g) mushrooms, sliced

2 tbsp (4 g) fresh rosemary

1 tsp fresh thyme

1 (14.5-oz [429-ml]) can stout beer

4 cups (960 ml) beef broth

2 tbsp (30 ml) Worcestershire sauce

1 (6-oz [177-ml]) can tomato paste

3 tbsp (24 g) cornstarch, mixed with 3 tbsp (45 ml) water

Chopped parsley, for garnish

TRADITIONAL IRISH STOUT STEW

Irish stout stew is traditionally served over mashed potatoes but takes forever to make! To save time and hassle, I made this recipe with the potatoes cooked right in. So when you're ready, it's ready!

1. Stir the meat, salt, pepper, pearl onions, white onion, celery, carrots, potatoes, mushrooms, rosemary and thyme together in your 6-quart (6-L) slow cooker.

2. Stir together the beer, broth, Worcestershire sauce and tomato paste in a large bowl. Pour the broth mixture into your slow cooker over the meat and vegetables, cover and cook on high for 4 hours or on low for 8 hours.

3. If cooking on low, turn your slow cooker to high, add the cornstarch mixture and stir. Cover and cook for another 20 minutes. Serve garnished with parsley.

CHICKEN POT PIE SOUP

Chicken pot pie is a classic family dinner, but who really has time to make the pie dough? Here it is made easier than ever as a delicious soup.

1. Combine the chicken, onion, celery, carrots, garlic, salt, pepper, thyme, broth and bay leaf in your 6-quart (6-L) slow cooker. Cover and cook on high for 4 hours or on low for 8 hours.

2. One hour before the cooking time is done, remove the bay leaf and stir in the cornstarch mixture and the peas. If cooking on low, turn your slow cooker to high, cover and continue to cook for the remaining hour. Remove the chicken and shred using two forks. Stir the chicken back into the soup and serve.

1½ lbs (681 g) boneless, skinless chicken thighs

1 medium onion, diced

3 ribs celery, diced

3 carrots, diced

1 clove garlic, minced

1½ tsp (9 g) salt

½ tsp pepper

1 tsp dried thyme

4 cups (960 ml) chicken broth

1 bay leaf

¼ cup (32 g) cornstarch, mixed with ¼ cup (60 ml) water

½ cup (67 g) frozen peas

¾ lb (340 g) smoked sausage, sliced ½ inch (1.3 cm) thick

1 yellow onion, diced

2 cloves garlic, minced

2 ribs celery, diced

1 green bell pepper, diced

2 tbsp (16 g) flour

1 (10-oz [283-g]) can diced tomatoes with green chilies, with liquid

½ cup (120 ml) water

2 cups (224 g) frozen sliced okra, thawed

¼ tsp cayenne pepper

1 tsp salt

½ lb (227 g) large shrimp, peeled and deveined

SAUSAGE AND SHRIMP CAJUN STEW

Deliciously savory with a bit of kick, this Cajun stew is perfect for the slow cooker. Just a few simple ingredients, and you're on your way to a delicious dinner.

1. Place the sausage, onion, garlic, celery and bell pepper in your 6-quart (6-L) slow cooker. Sprinkle in the flour and toss to coat. Add the tomatoes, water, okra, cayenne and salt. Cover and cook for 3½ hours on high or for 7 hours on low.

2. If cooking on low, turn your slow cooker to high, add the shrimp, cover and cook for 30 more minutes.

HOMINY, BEAN AND SAUSAGE SOUP

A deliciously hearty soup that's Mexican-inspired and loaded with protein-packed beans and vegetables. It can be served mild for a family-friendly dinner or hot for those who adore a nice kick in the taste buds.

1. Heat the oil in a large skillet over medium-high heat. Add the sausage and cook until no longer pink, for about 5 to 7 minutes. Add the sausage, onion, pinto beans, kidney beans, hominy, tomatoes, carrots, celery, red pepper, broth, garlic, salt, pepper and pepper flakes to your 6-quart (6-L) slow cooker and stir. Cover and cook on high for 3 hours or on low for 6 hours.

1 tsp oil

2 lbs (908 g) ground Italian sausage—mild or hot will work well here

1 medium onion, chopped

1 (15-oz [425-g]) can pinto beans, drained

1 (15-oz [425-g]) can kidney beans, drained

2 (15-oz [425-g]) cans hominy, drained

1 (15-oz [425-g]) can diced tomatoes

2 carrots, sliced

2 ribs celery, diced

1 red bell pepper, chopped

4 cups (960 ml) chicken broth

3 cloves garlic, minced

1 tsp salt

½ tsp pepper

1 tsp dried red pepper flakes, optional for more heat

REAL EASY

🍲 BBQ

Your slow cooker may not be the first thing that comes to mind when you think about barbecue, but that doesn't mean it's impossible! The two really can work together harmoniously. Sure, there are no smokers involved, but you can certainly produce fall-off-the-bone tender meats in your slow cooker. Browse through this next section and you will know this to be true!

TOP 5

- *Tender Shredded BBQ Pulled Pork (page 130)*
- *Sticky BBQ Pork Ribs (page 133)*
- *Brown Sugar Chili Bacon Meatballs (page 134)*
- *Zesty BBQ Pulled Chicken (page 139)*
- *Bacon Baked Beans (page 140)*

TENDER SHREDDED BBQ PULLED PORK

Nothing beats a slow-cooked pork that is fall-off-the-bone tender and juicy. Add barbecue sauce, and you have the perfect pairing for a meal. This pork is cooked right with the sauce, which makes this already easy dish even easier to make! Nothing says barbecue to me like a pulled pork sandwich.

1. Place the pork roast in your 6-quart (6-L) slow cooker.

2. Stir the BBQ sauce, vinegar and broth together in a medium bowl. Stir in the sugar, mustard, Worcestershire sauce, chili powder, onion, garlic and thyme. Pour the sauce mixture over the roast. Cover and cook on high for 4 hours or on low for 8 hours.

3. Carefully remove the roast from your slow cooker and shred the meat using two forks. Return the shredded pork to your slow cooker, stirring the meat into the juices.

SERVES 8

3 lbs (1.4 kg) pork shoulder roast

1 cup (240 ml) BBQ sauce—use sauce of choice

¼ cup (60 ml) apple cider vinegar

½ cup (120 ml) chicken broth

¼ cup (55 g) light brown sugar

1 tbsp (15 ml) prepared yellow mustard

1 tbsp (15 ml) Worcestershire sauce

1 tbsp (8 g) chili powder

1 large onion, diced

2 cloves garlic, crushed

1½ tsp (2 g) dried thyme

POACHING LIQUID

2 cups (480 ml) soy
sauce

4 cups (960 ml) water

¾ cup (165 g) brown
sugar

1 tbsp (15 ml) molasses

6 lbs (2.7 kg) pork ribs,
silver skin removed,
racks cut in half or
smaller to fit your slow
cooker

SAUCE

1 (12-oz [340-g]) bottle
chili sauce

14 oz (414 ml) ketchup

¾ cup (165 g) brown
sugar

1 tbsp (15 ml) prepared
yellow mustard

STICKY BBQ PORK RIBS

I grew up with my mom making these ribs every summer. She originally made them in a roaster, but they adapted perfectly for the slow cooker! These ribs are tender, savory and have the perfect BBQ sauce to accompany them.

1. Stir the soy sauce, water, sugar and molasses together in your 6-quart (6-L) slow cooker. Submerge the ribs into the poaching liquid, cover and cook on high for 6 hours or on low for 12 hours.

2. Bring the chili sauce, ketchup, sugar and mustard to a boil in a medium saucepan over medium-high heat and stir. Reduce the heat, cover and simmer for 30 minutes, stirring occasionally.

3. Once the ribs are done, remove them from your slow cooker. Transfer them to a broiler pan and brush with the sauce. Broil on high for 4 minutes, turn the ribs and brush with sauce. Repeat 3 more times per side.

BROWN SUGAR CHILI BACON MEATBALLS

This savory dish is a fun twist on meatballs that steps out quite a bit from its Italian roots. These meatballs are loaded up with bacon and a delicious BBQ sauce, which may sound odd but is actually extremely tasty!

1. Combine the bacon, onion, beef, breadcrumbs, salt, pepper, parsley, egg, garlic, mustard and Worcestershire sauce in a large bowl and mix just until incorporated—it is easiest, albeit a little messier, to use your hands to combine. Form the meat into 1½-inch (3.8-cm) balls and set aside—if the mixture is sticking to your hands, lightly moisten your hands with water, then continue rolling.

2. Stir the chili sauce, sugar and dressing in a medium bowl until smooth. Add half of the sauce mixture to the bottom of your 6-quart (6-L) slow cooker, place the meatballs in the sauce and top with the remaining sauce. Cook on high for 3 hours or on low for 6 hours.

SERVES 8

6 slices bacon, finely chopped or pulsed in a food processor

1 small onion, diced

2 lbs (908 g) ground beef

½ cup (68 g) breadcrumbs

1 tsp salt

¼ tsp pepper

½ cup (30 g) chopped fresh parsley

1 large egg, lightly beaten

3 cloves garlic, minced

2 tbsp (30 ml) Dijon mustard

1 tbsp (15 ml) Worcestershire sauce

SAUCE

¾ cup (180 ml) chili sauce

¾ cup (165 g) brown sugar

¾ cup (180 ml) whipped salad dressing (such as Miracle Whip)

DRY RUB BEEF BRISKET

Nothing says barbecue like a slow-cooked beef brisket. This may not be smoked for hours, but it's incredibly delicious on its own and is perfect for a quick dinner that tastes like you worked all day!

1. Line your 6-quart (6-L) slow cooker with a slow cooker bag. Stir the ketchup, sugar, water, onion, vinegar, Worcestershire sauce, garlic powder and pepper in a small bowl; set aside.

2. Add the paprika, chili powder, sugar, salt, garlic powder and pepper in another small bowl. Generously rub the brisket with the spice mixture and add the brisket to your slow cooker. Pour the sauce mixture over the brisket, cover and cook on high for 5 hours or on low for 10 hours.

3. Remove the brisket from your slow cooker, and slice across the grain into ¼-inch (0.6-cm) slices. Serve with the remaining sauce on top.

SERVES 12

SAUCE

1½ cups (360 ml) ketchup

½ cup (110 g) brown sugar

½ cup (120 ml) water

¼ cup (40 g) finely chopped yellow onion

3 tbsp (45 ml) apple cider vinegar

3 tbsp (45 ml) Worcestershire sauce

1 tsp garlic powder

¾ tsp pepper

BRISKET

¼ cup (27 g) sweet paprika

1 tbsp (8 g) chili powder

1 tbsp (14 g) brown sugar

1 tbsp (9 g) kosher salt, plus more as needed

1 tsp garlic powder

1 tsp pepper, plus more as needed

5 lbs (2.3 kg) beef brisket

1 cup (240 ml) ketchup

¼ cup (60 ml) honey

¼ cup (55 g) light brown sugar

¼ cup (60 ml) apple cider vinegar

½ cup (120 ml) water

1 tsp ground pepper

½ tbsp (4 g) onion powder

2 tsp (10 ml) lemon juice, about ½ lemon

1 tbsp (15 ml) Worcestershire sauce

8 bone-in, skinless chicken thighs

Prepared Texas toast, for serving

HONEY BBQ CHICKEN THIGHS

Chicken thighs are amazing in the slow cooker. They become extremely tender and are hard to overcook. Add this homemade honey barbecue sauce to take them to the next level. They are sticky good!

1. Stir the ketchup, honey, sugar, vinegar, water, pepper, onion powder, juice and Worcestershire sauce together in a large bowl. Add the chicken thighs and give them a toss.

2. Place the chicken in your 6-quart (6-L) slow cooker and pour any remaining sauce over the top. Cover and cook on high for 4 hours or on low for 8 hours. Serve over Texas toast.

ZESTY BBQ PULLED CHICKEN

1 cup (240 ml) ketchup

6 tbsp (90 ml) prepared yellow mustard

6 tbsp (84 g) brown sugar

2 tbsp (30 ml) Worcestershire sauce

2 cloves garlic, minced

1 small onion, minced

3 lbs (1.4 kg) chicken leg quarters, skin removed

Not far off from its pulled pork counterpart, this barbecue pulled chicken is really a great alternative. Give it a try—you might not even notice the difference!

1. Stir the ketchup, mustard, sugar, Worcestershire sauce, garlic and onion together in a medium bowl.

2. Remove any excess fat from the chicken. Place half of the chicken in the bottom of your 6-quart (6-L) slow cooker and pour half of the sauce over the top. Add the remaining chicken and cover completely with the remaining sauce. Cover and cook on high for 4 hours or on low for 8 hours—the meat should be tender enough that it will fall off the bone at this point.

3. Transfer the chicken to a plate. Pour the sauce from your slow cooker into a saucepan over medium heat and simmer until it has reduced by two-thirds. While the sauce is reducing, use two forks to pull the chicken from the bones and transfer to a large bowl. Add the reduced sauce to the pulled chicken and toss until the meat is thoroughly coated.

BACON BAKED BEANS

Here's another recipe from my family archives. My mother would make these beans every summer, and they are still a serious hit with just about everyone. You haven't tasted baked beans until you've had these baked beans!

1. Stir the beans, bacon, onion, sugar, ketchup, BBQ sauce, mustard and molasses together in your 6-quart (6-L) slow cooker. Cover and cook on high for 6 hours or on low for 12 hours.

6 (16-oz [454-g]) cans pork and beans, drained

6 slices bacon, cooked and crumbled—lean bacon bits work here

1 medium onion, finely diced

1 cup (220 g) brown sugar

1 cup (240 ml) ketchup

½ cup (120 ml) BBQ sauce—use your favorite here

1 tsp prepared yellow mustard

1 tbsp (15 ml) molasses

VEGETARIAN 🍲 DELIGHTS

Unfortunately, recipes that exclude meat have gotten a reputation as boring and flavorless. My goal with this section is to encourage you to expand your horizons and give meatless Monday a try! These recipes are a great introduction to a world where protein isn't limited to animals only. I love meat as much as anyone, but it can be fun to change it up!

MEXICAN QUINOA STUFFED PEPPERS

These Mexican-style stuffed peppers are loaded with quinoa and black beans, making them a vegetarian twist on the meat-filled classic. They are not only protein-packed but also incredibly filling.

1. Stir the quinoa, beans, tomatoes, onion, cumin, paprika, chili powder, garlic, pepper flakes, salt and pepper together in a large bowl. Evenly fill each pepper with the quinoa-bean mixture.

2. Add the water and tomato sauce to your 6-quart (6-L) slow cooker and stir. Place the stuffed peppers into the sauce, cover and cook on high for 3 hours or on low for 6 hours.

3. Carefully remove the peppers from your slow cooker, serve with the remaining sauce and topped with your desired toppings.

SERVES 6

1 cup (170 g) uncooked quinoa

1 (14.5-oz [411-g]) can black beans

1 (14.5-oz [411-g]) can diced tomatoes

1 medium onion, diced

2 tsp (6 g) ground cumin

1 tsp paprika

1 tsp chili powder

2 cloves garlic, minced

Red pepper flakes, to taste—optional if heat isn't your thing

1 tsp salt

½ tsp pepper

6 bell peppers, tops and seeds removed—orange, red or green work perfectly

½ cup (120 ml) water

1 (15-oz [425-g]) can tomato sauce

TOPPINGS

Green onions

Guacamole

Salsa

Fresh lime juice

Fresh cilantro

Shredded cheese

Sour cream

1¼ cups (300 ml) tomato sauce

1 tsp dried oregano

1 large eggplant or 2 medium, halved

2 tbsp (30 ml) oil

1 lb (454 g) portobello mushrooms, chopped

1 small onion, diced

2 cloves garlic, minced

Salt and pepper, to taste

½ cup (50 g) finely grated Parmesan cheese, plus more for serving

1 cup (56 g) panko breadcrumbs

1 egg, beaten

ITALIAN-SPICED STUFFED EGGPLANT

Eggplant is an ingredient every Italian knows well. They are more versatile than you think and are big enough to be filled with all sorts of goodies! Italian-inspired and loaded to the brim with nutritious portobello mushrooms, these stuffed eggplants won't leave you hungry.

1. Pour the tomato sauce into your 6-quart (6-L) slow cooker, sprinkle in the oregano and stir. Using a spoon, scoop out the flesh of the eggplant—leave about a ½-inch (1.3-cm) layer inside so the skins don't become too delicate. Dice the scooped-out flesh and set aside.

2. Heat the oil in a large skillet over medium-high heat. Add the mushrooms, onion and diced eggplant, cooking for about 6 to 8 minutes until the vegetables are tender. Stir in the garlic and cook for 1 more minute. Transfer the mixture to a large bowl, season with salt and pepper and stir in the Parmesan, breadcrumbs and the egg. Divide the mixture evenly into the eggplant halves.

3. Place the eggplants skin-side down into the sauce. Cover and cook on high for 3 hours or on low for 6 hours. Serve topped with the tomato sauce and grated Parmesan.

BLACK BEAN AND QUINOA ENCHILADA PIE

Vegetable lovers are crazy about enchiladas but don't have the time to roll them. If you know you have a long day ahead, this recipe will make dinner preparation a breeze. By the time you get home, this pie is done and ready to eat!

1. Heat the oil in a large skillet over medium-high heat. Add the onion, poblano, cumin, chili powder, salt and pepper and sauté for about 6 to 8 minutes, until tender. Stir in the garlic, quinoa and the water, cover and cook for 15 minutes, until the water is fully absorbed by the quinoa. Stir in the black beans, corn and tomatoes.

2. Using non-stick cooking spray, lightly coat your 4½- to 5-quart (4.5- to 5-L) slow cooker. Lay a tortilla in your slow cooker; cover with 1 cup (240 g) of the quinoa and bean mixture in a layer, sprinkle ¼ cup (28 g) cheese on top and repeat with the remaining tortillas, reserving some cheese for serving. Cover and cook on high for 3 hours or on low for 6 hours. Before serving, top with the remaining cheese, cilantro and sour cream.

SERVES 4

1 tbsp (15 ml) oil

1 medium onion, diced

1 poblano pepper, diced—poblano is not a spicy pepper but if you are looking for some extra heat, leave the seeds

2 tsp (6 g) ground cumin

1 tbsp (8 g) chili powder

1 tsp salt

1 tsp pepper

2 cloves garlic, minced

1 cup (170 g) uncooked quinoa

2 cups (480 ml) water

1 (14.5-oz [411-g]) can black beans, drained

1 (14-oz [397-g]) can corn, drained

1 (10-oz [283-g]) can diced tomatoes with chilies, with liquid

6 (6-inch [15-cm]) flour tortillas

2 cups (225 g) shredded cheese of choice

Fresh chopped cilantro, for garnish

Sour cream, for serving

CAULIFLOWER BOLOGNESE WITH ZUCCHINI NOODLES

While by no means a proper Italian Bolognese, this "meat" sauce is fit for vegetarians and non-vegetarians alike. I designed this recipe to mimic all the best parts of a slow-cooked sauce. If zucchini noodles aren't your thing, regular or wheat pasta will also pair well here.

SERVES 4

1 head cauliflower, cut up into florets

1 small red onion, diced

2 cloves garlic, minced

2 tsp (2 g) dried oregano

1 tsp dried basil

1 (14-oz [397-g]) can diced tomatoes

1 (14-oz [397-g]) can tomato sauce

½ cup (120 ml) vegetable broth

¼ tsp red pepper flakes—optional if heat isn't your thing

Salt and pepper, to taste

5 large zucchinis, zoodled or ribboned

1. Stir the cauliflower, onion, garlic, oregano, basil, tomatoes, sauce, broth, pepper flakes, salt and pepper together in your 6-quart (6-L) slow cooker. Cover and cook on high for 4 hours or on low for 8 hours.

2. When done cooking, mash the cauliflower with a potato masher or fork until the florets break up—this will create a chunky texture for a more authentic bolognese. Serve over zucchini noodles.

1 tbsp (15 ml) oil

2 lbs (908 g) fresh button mushrooms, trimmed and quartered

1 lb (454 g) fresh cremini mushrooms, quartered

1 medium onion, thinly sliced

4 cloves garlic, minced

½ cup (64 g) flour

1 cup (240 ml) vegetable broth

1 tbsp (15 ml) Worcestershire sauce

Salt and pepper, to taste

12 oz (340 g) egg noodles

⅓ cup (80 ml) sour cream

1½ tbsp (23 ml) Dijon mustard

½ cup (4 g) fresh dill, chopped

MUSHROOM-LOADED STROGANOFF

When you don't eat meat, you may feel like you miss out on some really good comfort dishes. Well luckily for you, stroganoff is now a meal vegetarians can happily welcome to the table. Plus, mushrooms are vitamin-packed and loaded with flavor! This recipe is so good you'll be asking yourself, "Who needs meat anyway?"

1. Heat the oil in a large skillet over medium-high heat. Sauté the button and cremini mushrooms, onion and garlic—to remove their liquid—for about 5 to 7 minutes. Stir in the flour, cooking for another 2 to 3 minutes, stirring constantly—this is to avoid the possibility of burning the flour.

2. Transfer the mushroom mixture to your 6-quart (6-L) slow cooker. Gradually pour in the broth and the Worcestershire sauce. Stir in the salt and pepper, cover and cook on high for 4 hours or low for 8 hours.

3. Cook the noodles according to the package directions. Stir the sour cream and mustard into your slow cooker and serve over the noodles topped with fresh dill.

2 (14.5-oz [411-g]) cans black beans, drained

2 cups (480 ml) vegetable broth

2 (14-oz [397-g]) cans diced tomatoes

1 medium onion, diced

1 green bell pepper, diced

1 jalapeño pepper, seeded and minced, optional for added heat

2 medium sweet potatoes, peeled and diced

2 tbsp (11 g) cocoa powder—sounds odd, but it adds richness

1 tbsp (8 g) chili powder

2 tsp (6 g) ground cumin

½ tsp paprika

¼ tsp cayenne pepper—more or less to taste

1 tsp salt

½ cup (85 g) uncooked quinoa

OPTIONAL TOPPINGS

Cilantro

Greek yogurt or vegan sour cream

Shredded cheese

Chopped green onions

BLACK BEAN AND SWEET POTATO CHILI

Chili is a meal that I never get tired of cooking because there are so many variations. The sweet potatoes add a unique flavor that most chilies don't have. This meatless option is spicy, savory and full of fantastic vegetarian nutrition.

1. Stir the beans, broth, tomatoes, onion, bell and jalapeño peppers, sweet potatoes, cocoa, chili powder, cumin, paprika, cayenne and salt together in your 6-quart (6-L) slow cooker. Cover and cook on high for 4 hours or on low for 8 hours.

2. Add the quinoa to your slow cooker. If cooking on low, turn your slow cooker to high, cover and cook for 1 more hour—alternatively, the quinoa can be added 1 hour before it's done. Before serving, stir and serve with assorted toppings.

SPRING VEGETABLE FRITTATA

Frittatas are a perfect excuse to eat eggs for dinner. Convenient, full of protein and not to mention very budget friendly, this is one way to use up some extras you have in the refrigerator. If you've never had a frittata, think something along the lines of an omelet that serves more people.

SERVES 4

1 tsp olive oil

4 oz (113 g) mushrooms, sliced

¼ cup (37 g) cherry tomatoes, sliced or quartered

2 green onions, sliced

¼ cup (8 g) fresh spinach, chopped

6 eggs

½ cup (57 g) shredded cheddar cheese

1 tbsp (6 g) Parmesan cheese

2 tsp (5 g) Italian seasoning

1. Using non-stick cooking spray, lightly coat your 4½- to 5-quart (4.5- to 5-L) slow cooker.

2. Heat the oil in a large skillet over medium-high heat. Add the mushrooms, tomatoes, onions and spinach and cook for about 4 minutes or until the spinach has wilted. Transfer the vegetables to your slow cooker.

3. Whisk together the eggs, cheddar and Parmesan cheese and Italian seasoning in a medium bowl. Pour the egg mixture over the vegetables, cover and cook on high for 2 hours or on low for 4 hours.

4 medium sweet
potatoes, washed

½ cup (120 g) canned
black beans, drained

½ cup (83 g) corn, fresh
or frozen

⅓ cup (80 ml) canned
tomato sauce

2 tbsp (12 g) green
onion, chopped

½ tsp ground cumin

¼ tsp cayenne pepper

½ tsp salt

1 avocado, chopped

2 tbsp (2 g) chopped
cilantro

TEX-MEX SWEET POTATOES

Sweet potatoes may not be the first thing that comes to mind as a main course, but they are packed with vitamins and are delicious. Loading them up with satisfying fillings rounds these Tex-Mex delights off as a perfect dinner for any day of the week!

1. Place the sweet potatoes in your 6-quart (6-L) slow cooker, cover and cook on high for 3 hours or low for 6 hours.

2. Stir together the beans, corn, sauce, onion, cumin, cayenne and salt in a medium saucepan over medium-high heat. Cook 5 to 10 minutes or until heated through.

3. Remove the potatoes from your slow cooker and cut each lengthwise three-fourths of the way through. Pull apart to create an opening and gently mash the flesh with a fork. Evenly fill each potato with the bean mixture. Serve with avocado and cilantro on top.

INDIAN-SPICED VEGETABLE CURRY

They say curry is a food that warms your belly first, then your heart. In this vegetarian version, simple ingredients come together to make a delicious dinner that's satisfying and beautifully colored. Try this easy dish and put a little warmth in your belly.

1. Add the cauliflower, bell pepper, onion, sweet potatoes and chickpeas to your 6-quart (6-L) slow cooker.

2. Stir the broth, garlic, curry powder and tomato puree together in a medium bowl. Pour the mixture over the vegetables and stir. Cover and cook on high for 4 hours or on low for 8 hours.

3. Prepare the rice according to package directions. Stir the coconut milk into your slow cooker and season with salt and pepper. Serve over rice.

SERVES 6

1 large head cauliflower, cut into bite-sized pieces

1 red bell pepper, thinly sliced

1 small onion, chopped

2 large sweet potatoes, peeled and chopped

1 (15-oz [425-g]) can chickpeas, drained

2 cups (480 ml) vegetable broth

2 cloves garlic, minced

2 tbsp (13 g) curry powder

1 cup (240 ml) tomato puree

2 cups (370 g) uncooked Basmati rice

1 (14-oz [414-ml]) can unsweetened coconut milk

Salt and pepper, to taste

ACKNOWLEDGMENTS

The idea of even trying to express the amount of gratitude I have, in writing, is actually quite daunting, but I do think it's necessary to thank these people:

To my parents, for the love and support of this millennial pursuing his dreams. Thank you for allowing me to destroy your kitchen and for the use of the cooking appliances I would be doomed without. Mom, thank you for being my backbone in the photography world, for always being my shoulder to lean on and for all the help along the way, no matter what I needed.

To my sister—my fellow dreamer. When I told her this book was becoming a reality, the first thing she said was, "When do we start?" That "we" sums up exactly who she is. She has always been there for me with her sleeves rolled up to help, and for that, I could never put into words how much I appreciate her.

To Dallyn Maresco, you've been a huge support in just about every project I have taken on and this book was no exception. Thank you for being there through thick and thin, being my emotional as well as literal support. I couldn't ask for a better partner in crime.

To my grandma, although you will never read this, this book came to be because of you. You expressed your love through the kitchen and the food that came out of it. I wouldn't trade those countless memories in the kitchen with you for anything in the world. Love you and miss you.

To my fellow foodie Melanie Stansbury, thank you for being my culinary friend. Thank you for always being there for support and for allowing me to bounce my culinary ideas off of you.

To Page Street, for this amazing opportunity to become a book author and for taking a chance on me. To Marissa Giambelluca, for being the biggest help as my liaison and coordinator within the publishing world. You have made this adventure very enjoyable.

And to the wonderful people who tried every recipe and gave their honest (and sometimes too honest) feedback: Bobbi and Travis Bohan, Katie Decker, Rachel Cormany, Michelle Hill, Jillian Maresco, Marcia Pelione and Heather Robles.

ABOUT THE AUTHOR

Drew Maresco is the founder and editor-in-chief of the popular website and magazine BestRecipes.co. He is a self-taught cook with a mind for creating unique and delicious recipes. For Drew, inspiration began at a young age, sitting atop his grandmother's kitchen counter as she let him assist with everything she baked. From there he developed into a foodie with an entrepreneurial mindset and a big appetite, and even bigger dreams. Drew dove headfirst into the culinary world and owned his first business at age nineteen. From humble beginnings, he created his first food blog, and a starter website which has evolved into the ever-growing brand and publication he now runs. Drew has a knack for taking a few simple ingredients and turning them into something unique and interesting, while making it accessible to all. This is his first cookbook, which adds to the collection of recipes Drew has created and made available to a hungry audience—both in print (in his own magazine publications) as well as in the form of tutorial videos. He has also published recipes in various local magazines.

Drew was born and raised in the culturally diverse Detroit area, which expanded his culinary palate by giving him access to the foods from these cultures and the opportunity to learn cooking styles from a variety of backgrounds and heritages. Enjoying new food and drink everywhere he goes is a simple delight for him and living in a reviving area like Metro Detroit (where restaurants are popping up constantly) makes every day a new food adventure as he decides which cuisine to try.

INDEX